WALLS
ARE
TALKING
WALLPAPER, ART AND CULTURE

Published in the UK by
The Whitworth Art Gallery
The University of Manchester
Oxford Road, Manchester M15 6ER
www.manchester.ac.uk/whitworth

In association with
KWS Publishers
1516 North State Parkway
Chicago, Illinois 60610, USA

or

11 Tower House
Candover Street
London W1W 7DQ, UK
www.kwspub.com

Published to coincide with the exhibition
Walls Are Talking: Wallpaper, Art and Culture
5 February–3 May 2010
The Whitworth Art Gallery
The University of Manchester

© the artists, authors, The Whitworth Art Gallery
and KWS Publishers

ISBN: 978-0-9842260-0-9 (KWS)
ISBN: 978-0-903261-65-4 (The Whitworth)

Acknowledgements
The authors are indebted to many people for their
support, advice and expert knowledge in the
research, writing and production of this book. In
particular we would like to thank the artists,
designers and manufacturers whose work is featured
here and from whom we have learned so much in
the course of correspondence and conversation. We
would also like to thank curatorial colleagues past
and present for sharing their insights and expertise,
in particular Rosie Miles (V&A), and Jennifer Harris
(Whitworth), who also read early drafts of the text,
and offered valuable constructive criticism.

Many people have contributed significantly to the
production and design of the book. Special thanks
must go to Daniel Kirkpatrick of KWS, for his
expeditious and exacting editorial input; also to
Hannah Brookfield (Whitworth) who undertook most
of the picture research and cleared copyright for the
illustrations with despatch and good humour; and to
Roxanne Peters (V&A Images) who facilitated our use
of the images of material from the V&A collections.
We are immensely grateful to Shawn Stipling, the
designer, for his patience in the face of sporadic
delivery of the contents and many thanks are also
due to Frank Cockerill and Dr Alfonso Ciotola of
Dresden Papier GmbH for their enthusiastic
involvement in this project. Finally, it would have
been impossible to achieve this book and the
exhibition it accompanied without the financial
support of the North West Regional Development
Agency's 'Raising the Game' initiative.

Gill Saunders and Christine Woods would also like to
thank their partners, Shaie Selzer and David Greysmith,
for their practical support and advice throughout.

Designed by aquarium 01371 831644. aquariumgd.co.uk
Cover designed by Creative Concern
Printed by Butler Tanner & Dennis Fine Art Services

ENDPAPERS: Rosemarie Trockel, *Egg Curtain* wallpaper/poster
1998. Offset lithograph © Rosemarie Trockel, VG Bild-Kunst,
Bonn 2009. Courtesy Sprüth Magers, Berlin, London

WALLS ARE TALKING

WALLPAPER, ART AND CULTURE

Gill Saunders

Dominique Heyse-Moore

Trevor Keeble

with an introduction by Christine Woods

The University of Manchester
The Whitworth Art Gallery

CHICAGO • LONDON

Contents

Director's Foreword

The wallpaper collection at the Whitworth is one of our unusual treasures. That there should be a wallpaper collection, and for that matter a world textile collection, within what otherwise might appear to be a fine art institution is testament to the vision of the Whitworth founders and to our Manchester location. Wallpapers became firmly a part of the Whitworth's collection with a large donation in 1967, from the Wall Paper Manufacturers Ltd, which donated its extensive archive to the gallery in recognition of the importance of the North West in the production of domestic wallpapers. Since that time, the Collection has developed to encompass wallcoverings produced across more than three centuries, including all aspects of wallpaper manufacture from mainstream commercial designs to those made as fine art works by individual artists.

This publication, which acts as a companion text to our exhibition *Walls Are Talking: Wallpaper, Art and Culture*, makes an exuberant argument for the destabilizing impact of this usually domestic medium in the hands of artists and designers who generally live in a fine art world. By misbehaving as art object and domestic decoration the works in this show expose themselves and critique the social and cultural mores of the society within which they are produced. Seriously playful, as the essays in this publication demonstrate, these wallpapers seduce and challenge in equal measure.

This catalogue and exhibition have been made possible through a richly rewarding collaboration with the Victoria and Albert Museum, the curatorial knowledge and extensive collections of which have been drawn on in the development and realization of this project. The exhibition and publication are exemplary models of partnership between national and regional collections. Great thanks are due to Gill Saunders, Senior Curator of Prints at the V&A, and also to Julius Bryant and Mark Jones at the V&A for facilitating their curator to work on this Whitworth project. Publications and exhibitions are significant intellectual endeavours as well as resource-intensive projects, so thanks go to Dresden Papier GmbH and the North West Regional Development Agency for support that has made the publication possible, and to Gill Saunders, Christine Woods, Dominique Heyse-Moore and Trevor Keeble, whose labour has brought it to fruition.

Maria Balshaw
Director, The Whitworth Art Gallery, The University of Manchester

OPPOSITE:
Francesco Simeti, *Arabian Nights* [detail], 2003 [Plate 40]

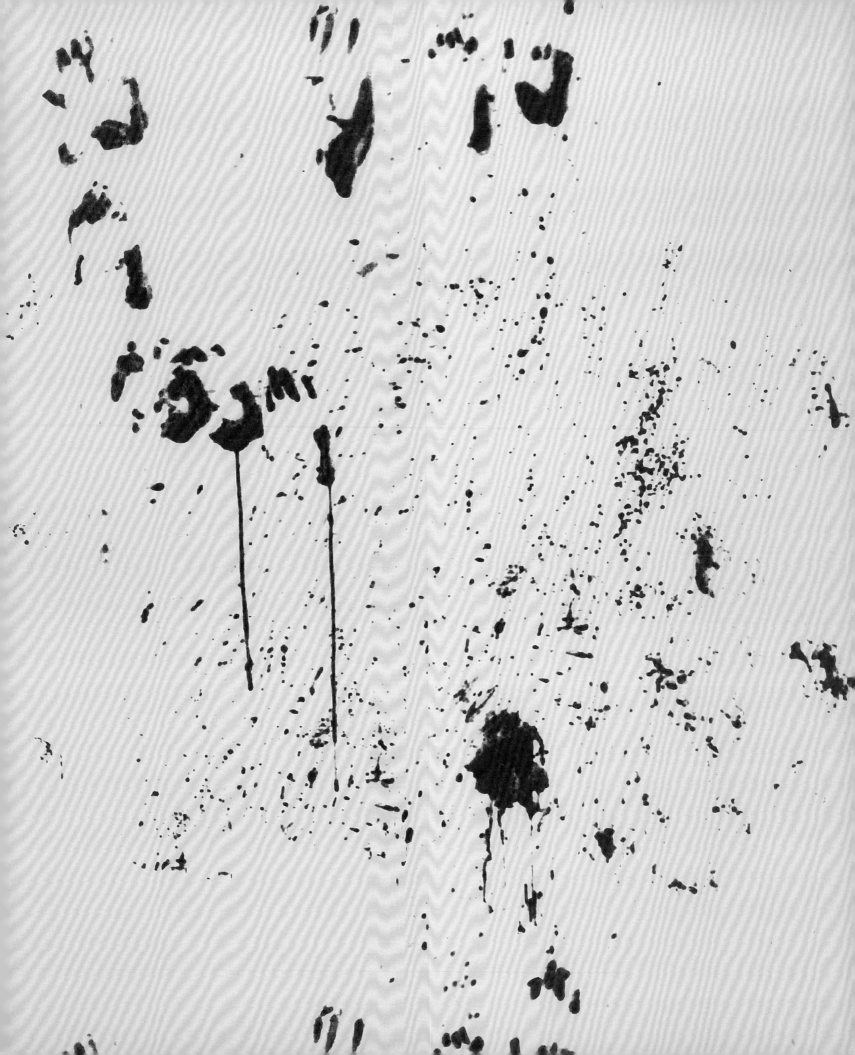

Preface

Consumers are usually primarily concerned with the pattern on their wallpaper, but the quality of the product is largely determined by the paper substrate. It must withstand the printing process, hold the colours and lend itself to being rolled and then hung on a wall – it must not, for example, stretch like a tea-bag when wet. Also, of course, it must survive in a variety of domestic, corporate and, these days, as this book shows, art gallery environments.

Initially a craft skill carried out by artisans in small workshops, paper manufacture is now a major high-tech industry. The Saxony region of Germany has a long tradition of paper-making and Dresden Papier GmbH, located in Heidenau, is a historic firm that is developing new products in response to renewed consumer interest in wallcoverings and the consequent explosion of new ideas. As a result, we have moved away from standard paper production to the manufacture of a new product, 'non-woven' paper, which is dimensionally stable and, because it involves pasting the wall, has made paperhanging much easier. It appeals in particular to a generation that prefers quick and easy decorating solutions, since its characteristics make possible a perfect finish every time.

Dresden Papier is known mainly for its production of many varieties of non-woven paper for the wallcoverings industry but many of the contemporary artists whose works are illustrated in this book have also used this type of paper. Traditionally the relationship between art and industry has been somewhat uncomfortable, but the recognition that wallpaper is now a legitimate medium for the expression of artistic ideas gives one hope for the future. For that reason Dresden Papier is pleased to be able to support this publication.

Dr Alfonso Ciotola
CEO, Dresden Papier GmbH

Introduction: 'It's the background that explains the foreground'[1]

BELOW:

1. Front cover of a wallpaper pattern book issued by S. M. Bryde & Co., Leeds, 1895. The Whitworth Art Gallery, The University of Manchester, W.1991.7

The decoration of domestic interiors with wallpaper has been common practice for more than 200 years and it has supported substantial industries in Europe and America. That the wallpaper industry's fortunes have fluctuated with fashion is not surprising – according to one authority, wallpapers are selected because they are 'new' and 'different' and 'pretty'.[2] Wallpapers designed by artists, which are the main focus of this book, are, however, rarely pretty. Their motifs are often arranged in familiar patterns, but they speak a different language and subvert wallpaper's traditional function as innocuous background to daily life – although, in fact, wallpaper has rarely been just background. While wallpapers by contemporary artists proclaim their subversive intention, domestic wallcoverings have always had a more covert influence.

This introduction describes the (often contradictory) relationship between art, wallpaper and the consumer, and questions the perceived neutrality of our papered walls.

The association of wallpaper with art has traditionally been regarded as impossible, a contradiction in terms. In Western culture the fine arts (painting, sculpture, architecture) have generally been accorded higher status than the decorative arts and, compared to that of designers, the position of artists has been similarly elevated. In 1839 *The Art-Union*, 'a monthly journal of the fine arts', bemoaned the superiority of French wallpapers over English and stated that 'Art must be called in'. 'Surely', the anonymous author wrote, 'good artists may be found in England who will stoop (?) to lend assistance to such undertakings!'[3] A few artists did just that, but, as one of their number remarked, the whole idea of 'the mechanical reproduction of any form of art wholesale was a mistake'.[4] In the late 18th and 19th centuries efforts were made by French and English manufacturers to raise the status of wallpaper to that of fine art. In France artists were frequently employed to work on scenic and other wallpaper decorations[5] and by the 1880s the term 'artistic' was being

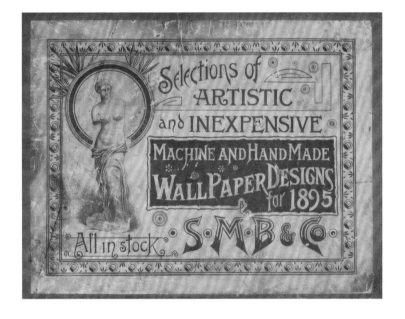

applied to English wallpapers at every level of the market. In order to reinforce the association of their wallpapers with art, manufacturers and distributors routinely used images of, for example, the artist's palette or the Venus de Milo on their pattern books and advertising [Plate 1]. Although this marketing strategy was useful until about 1900, ultimately it was doomed, not least because individual wallpapers cannot exhibit the 'aura of authorship' required of a work of art.[6] Wallpapers might have been touched by the hand of a craftsman, but, until recently, rarely by that of an artist – although they have often been depicted in works of art, for example by the painter Edouard Vuillard[7] [Plates 2 and 3]. In one notable instance actual wallpaper was used by Picasso as a major component in a collage, *Femmes à leur toilette*, of 1938 [Plate 4], but, in terms of commercial production, the relationship between art and industry was considered to be at best a 'mariage de convenance'.[8] This

view was reinforced by the Surrealist painter René Magritte, who, having worked for a short time in a Belgian wallpaper factory, insisted that, for artists, the decorative arts kill 'pure' art.[9]

The categorization and consequent denigration of wallpaper as one of the decorative arts seems to have held sway until 1966, when Andy Warhol produced his *Cow* wallpaper and, in 1974, his *Mao*. By then one of Germany's major wallpaper manufacturers, Marburger, had issued a collection of wallpapers designed by specially commissioned artists whose work was more usually produced as 'one-off' artworks. Included were the Swiss sculptor Jean Tinguely, the French artist Niki de Saint Phalle and the English 'Pop Artist' Peter Phillips. But these examples were, for the most part, pictorial rather than floral and depicted non-traditional subject matter represented in unusual ways [Plate 5].

ABOVE: **2.** Edouard Vuillard (1868–1940), *Woman in Blue with a Child*, c.1899. Oil on cardboard. Glasgow Art Gallery and Museum, Kelvingrove. Photo: Culture and Sport Glasgow (Museums)/© ADAGP, Paris and DACS, London 2009. The woman pictured is Misia Natanson, Vuillard's lover and muse.

LEFT: **3.** Art Nouveau wallpaper, c.1895–98. Manufacturer unknown. Musée du Papier Peint, Rixheim (France), Coll. Claude Frères 1898. This wallpaper is an important element of the *mise en scène* in several of Vuillard's paintings of Misia Natanson.

Ranges of this kind were never regarded as products for the mainstream. They were special, produced at considerable expense to maintain the reputation of Marburger as manufacturers of products for elite consumers, although the bulk of its production was directed at the general, more conservative market.

Since the 1990s, however, avant-garde artists have been using wallpaper increasingly to explore themes of home, memory and identity, often using papered walls to both encapsulate and reinforce their ideas. Some have used wallpaper as pictorial polemic by illustrating, for example, warfare or racism [Plate 6], others have made visually obvious the conflicts in contemporary Western culture, in particular those associated with gender and sexuality. The employment in such a way of what is generally regarded as an item of domestic

decoration or the butt of jokes [Plate 7] is an interesting phenomenon, not least because it has influenced the commercial wallpaper industry, which, in addition to continuing production largely for traditional markets, has kept a keen eye on recent trends. It could be argued that the relationship between these two very different aspects of wallpaper, although apparently symbiotic, is, in fact, parasitic – the larger, more conservative sector adapting and, perhaps more important, diluting new ideas for its own ends.

Perhaps the conflicts of interest inherent in this relationship mirror long-standing contradictions in the dealings between consumers and wallpaper itself. Wallpaper rarely hits the headlines. It is generally regarded as 'merely' decorative, an innocuous backdrop to our lives. It is commonplace; its very ubiquity renders it invisible. But, in effect, in its

OPPOSITE:
4. Pablo Picasso, *Femmes à leur toilette*, 1938. Collage of wallpaper. Musée Picasso, Paris. Photo: Réunion des Musées Nationaux © Succession Picasso/DACS 2009

BELOW:
5. Peter Phillips, *Kenya*, 1972. Machine-printed wallpaper. Manufactured by Marburger Tapetenfabrik GmbH. The Whitworth Art Gallery, The University of Manchester, W.1986. 5

domestic incarnation, wallpaper softens, humanizes. In choosing wallpaper the consumer is laying claim to being part of the civilized world. Nowhere was this more apparent than in the timber shacks that served as homes for emigrants to 19th-century Australia, where the incongruous presence of wallpaper symbolized the settlers' control over their environment. In papering over the cracks, wallpaper helped to satisfy a need for respectable gentility – and helped to hold the Empire together.[10] At home, in Britain, wallpaper enabled the middle and lower-middle classes to distance themselves (in every sense) from the slum dwellings of the dirty poor, which – paradoxically – were often hung with wallpaper that was once as pristine, albeit not as expensive, as their own.

Wallpaper is usually promoted solely as an item of fashionable taste, a means by which consumers can make an 'individual statement' about their own style and the way they like to live,[11] but its power extends far beyond attempts to express individuality. Wallpaper obliterates the past. It covers up the cracks, the dirt, the evidence. It wipes the slate clean, and enables new beginnings. One of the first things a new homeowner does is make their mark by redecorating, a form of taking control. At the height of the influence of Modernism the majority of English and American houses still had wallpaper, even if, like those produced from the Bauhaus designs, the wallpapers were almost invisible.[12] But wallpaper's benefits bring enormous pressure both to consume and to conform. In the act of decorating the consumer exhibits their class, status, and cultural affiliations. Wallpaper is not neutral.

For this reason, although inherently ephemeral and seen as a minor player on the decorative arts stage, wallpaper has played a crucial role in Western culture, not least in literature and painting, in which it has been used to conjure atmosphere, create mood and recall memories. For example, G.F. Green brings into sharp focus the oppressive intimacy of working-class life in a mining community as members of a tired

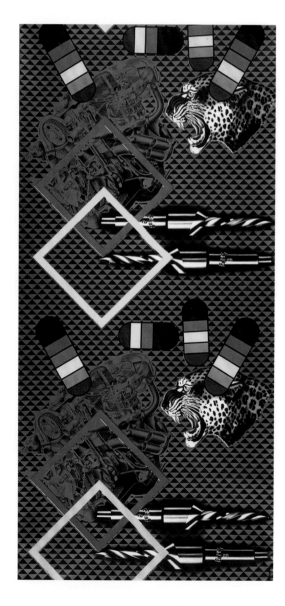

"The wallpaper looks very nice John, but what are all those bumps?"
"Good gracious, I forgot to take the pictures down!"

family eat, surrounded (enclosed?) by 'the patterned walls and ticking clock of the kitchen … '.[13] In contrast, the writer Leigh Hunt, writing retrospectively about his imprisonment, recalled how he was able to transcend his surroundings by papering the walls 'with a trellis of roses'.[14]

Compared to other decorative commodities wallpaper has a relatively recent history, but it has been an important signifier of social and fashionable status since the 18th century. By 1800 its manufacture had become a substantial industry, and it could be found decorating walls from Boston to Brussels. Mme de Pompadour had wallpapers in her wardrobe and passage at Versailles and Queen Charlotte used them in the Queen's Lodge, Windsor. Wallpapers proliferated in the dwellings of 'ordinary people', such as clergymen, as well as in grand houses. They were noted in hotels in Europe, and were both made in and imported into America. The poet and philosopher Goethe was delighted with 'the endless variety' produced in his friend's Frankfurt wallpaper factory, and in France wallpaper manufacturers employed many hundreds of people producing wallpapers for every section of the market.[15]

Initially, printed papers were seen as novelties, used to decorate the interiors of boxes and cupboards rather than entire rooms, but, as the range of products increased, wallpaper became a major component of the decorator's repertoire and decisions about the correct choice became crucial. In 1787, for example, a young man charged with papering his future home in Boston, Massachusetts, was 'totally at a loss what kind to get'[16] and the manager of sugar plantations in Grenada, preparing his new home in Scotland in 1789, asked the cabinetmaker Thomas Chippendale the Younger to choose the paper because he was a better judge of what was 'proper for a room'.[17] Thus, by the end of the 18th century, the choosing of wallpaper had become a source of concern rather than an entirely pleasurable activity.

This anxiety intensified during the 19th century. When mechanization of the wallpaper industry in the 1840s enabled a dramatic increase in production, lowering prices and bringing wallpaper within the reach of all but the very poor, a number of authorities on design expressed the view that concentration on machine production had caused a drop in standards. In addition to bemoaning the poor or non-existent training of designers, they castigated consumers for having low expectations. For these 'design reformers' the decoration of the majority of suburban and, indeed, town homes was regarded as one step away from barbarism.[18] To a large extent it was women who bore the brunt of the criticism. In middle- and lower-middle-class circles it was their responsibility to contribute to the status and comfort of the household by making correct decorative choices and providing a welcoming hearth for husband and family. Indeed, W.J. Loftie, in *A Plea for Art in the House*, wrote that the cultivation of taste was almost a religious duty as well as a moral one.[19] Matters of taste were discussed widely and a wealth of advice was available in journals aimed at professional decorators and in women's magazines, such as the *Lady's World* and *Ladies Realm*. The attitudes of the design reformers were parodied in several publications, including a story in *Household Words* in 1852, in which a Mr Crumpet visits the Museum of Ornamental Art and acquires 'Correct Principles of Taste', which lead him to believe that his house is full of 'horrors', in particular the wallpaper in his parlour, which is exuberant with birds of paradise, bridges and pagodas. A similar parody some two decades later detailed how an anonymous member of the Society of Arts was left a broken man by the realization that his wallpaper, which 'pretended to be the trellis-work of a summer arbour, with tropical plants creeping round it', was an abomination.[20] Nevertheless, middle-class consumers who preferred their wallpaper to exhibit realistic depictions of motifs of this kind, but who were told such designs were beyond the pale, must have been somewhat perplexed. Such anxieties were largely restricted to those whose social aspirations required them to keep up with the latest aesthetic pronouncements, but they are, nevertheless, a sign that wallpaper was being regarded increasingly as an indicator of membership of a social and cultural elite.

It might also send one mad.

Pattern, it was thought, influences the nervous system, and might act injuriously upon the mind, distracting feverish patients and giving rise to delirious fancies. When choosing the bedroom wallpaper, for example, it was important that '… care should be taken… to avoid any outré forms which the eye of a restless invalid, condemned to many hours of solitude, could torture into a form or a face of demon or grotesque horror.'[21] Those of nervous temperament could be irritated by badly defined patterns, which could also conjure up fantasies in the active minds of children. Small, distinctly outlined patterns could be equally problematic: they offered the eye no rest and produced mental effects that reacted on the whole system, annoying the restless at night and having a 'ghastly and nightmare' effect on the brain. According to one anecdote, it was possible to 'suffer beyond endurance' as a result of a design on a wallpaper.[22] This condition was memorably evoked by Charlotte Perkins Gilman in her 1892 story 'The Yellow Wallpaper', which chronicles her depressed character's obsession with a wallpaper pattern while she is confined/imprisoned in her room at the top of the house. Gilman's description is both vivid and chilling: 'it is stripped off … in great patches …The colour is repellent, almost revolting; a smouldering unclean yellow, strangely faded by the slow-turning sunlight …In the places where it isn't faded and where the sun is just so – I can see a strange, provoking, formless sort of figure, that seems to skulk about …'[23].

However, the cultural context of the debate about wallpaper was not solely related to matters of taste. Society was pervaded by anxiety about contamination of all kinds, such as the adulteration of foods and the corruption of society in general. This atmosphere provided fertile ground for worries about the presence of arsenic in wallpapers: its use was widespread. Although it was often supposed to be restricted to the production of emerald green, arsenic could be detected in many other colours used in the production of printed papers, and in numerous domestic fabrics and general consumables, ranging from cracker boxes and children's picture books to artificial flowers and labels on canned foods. Arsenic was employed at every level of the market because, it was said, arsenite of copper gave a brilliancy and permanency of colour unattainable by other means.[24]

Amounts varied. A small bedroom, having about 500 square feet (46.5 square metres) of wallpaper, could have 20,000 grains of arsenic on the walls. How dangerous was this? The medicinal dose of arsenic varied from one-sixteenth to one-twelfth of a grain, but medicine would be taken by mouth, whereas the cause of arsenical poisoning from wallpaper was generally thought to be either ingestion into the lungs – via the liberation of the colouring matter as dust – or inhalation of arseniuretted hydrogen, formed by chemical action on the salt of decomposing size and paste on damp walls.

There were numerous anecdotes about illnesses that had been traced to arsenical wallpapers, although there was some debate about this and more than one authority suggested that wallpaper was often blamed when conventional diagnosis failed. (However much we might delight in the knowledge that English wallpaper finally did for Napoleon, it is far more likely that cancer and frequent enemas were a major cause of his death.)[25] Nevertheless, the catalogue of possible symptoms was enough to put anybody off: ranging from slight inflammation of the eyes and a runny nose, to collapse, to convulsions ending in death.[26]

But assurances that wallpaper was free from arsenic – even if accurate – were no cause for complacency [Plate 8]. Decomposition of the paste

9. Wallpaper panel, French, c.1793. Hand-printed from woodblocks. Coll. Musée du Papier Peint, Rixheim (France), inv. 985 PP 3–10. This wallpaper features traditional symbols of the sovereign state, including the scales of justice, alongside revolutionary symbols such as the tricolour rosette and ribbon.

used in hanging wallpaper might cause an outbreak of 'malignant fever'.[27] If the fever did not arise from putrid paste, it might be caused by the tendency of wallpaper, because of its absorbent nature, to take in and give out 'atmospheric or gaseous products', which included 'vitiated germs' generated in heated atmospheres. And, of course, wallpapers, flocks in particular, attract and retain dust. Dust might be thought fairly innocuous, but, having examined it under the microscope, one turn-of-the-century authority described it thus:

soot, mineral particles (sand, crystals of sodium chloride), cotton fibres, spores of fungi or bacteria, starch grains, pulverized straw [and] *epithelial and epidermic debris from the skin.*

The writer went on to say that dust could be seen 'to consist largely of organic refuse, often more or less putrescent' and that 'nearly every part of a room is a dust trap'. This situation was made worse if the room was hung with 'rough or flock wallpapers'.[28]

In the light of these fears, it is, perhaps, no surprise that our relationship with wallpaper has often been uneasy. Indeed, although there are numerous versions of Oscar Wilde's deathbed pronouncement of 1900, his meaning is clear – wallpaper is dangerous.[29]

Is this still the case? We might say that our wallpaper is driving us mad, but this is not meant literally. Are 21st-century consumers in danger of being poisoned by their wallpaper? In 1932 it was reported that there was still a 'widespread belief' that wallpaper was a possible source of arsenic poisoning,[30] but this threat is no longer real. By the mid-1990s efforts were being made by some manufacturers to ensure that the production of wallcoverings avoided PVC, chlorine, toxic softeners, solvents, heavy metals, formaldehyde or CFCs.[31] Indeed, the use of vinyl wallcoverings in domestic environments is diminishing rapidly in the US and the use of

solvent-based printing inks is no longer popular in the industry generally. Owing to the installation of double glazing and more efficient draughtproofing, consumers still have to contend with mould and mildew, which thrive in houses where air circulation has been minimized, and anti-fungicide in paste becomes ineffective when it is sandwiched between two sealed layers.[32] However, these are not lethal situations.

The real threat posed by wallpaper is the result of its ability to reflect cultural patterns and, in doing so, to reinforce them. Wallpapers are as much the result of our cultural preoccupations as paintings and sculpture, and can often reveal more about a society's mood. But is what wallpapers reveal only what we choose to display?

Throughout its history wallpaper has most commonly been decorated with repeating patterns of floral or geometric motifs, but the designer's repertoire has always included pictorial or other 'novelty' decorations, and by the 1880s these began to be regularly included in manufacturers' ranges (usually intended for children, whose education and moral development, it was said, could be enhanced by the right kind of wallpaper[33]). In 19th-century France scenic and other wallpapers commemorating famous battles, such as Austerlitz, and, indeed, the Revolution, were not unusual [Plate 9]; pictorial representations of North America, including the port of Boston, were also produced by French manufacturers for export to the US. In England population growth and rising incomes encouraged an increase in the variety of consumer goods, and Victorians were encouraged to acquire mementos of political leaders or national events, which resulted in the production of a wide variety of commemorative objects. These social changes coincided with the introduction of technology that, by the 1880s, enabled the printing on wallpaper of finely detailed images similar to those we expect today. By the beginning of the 20th century numerous cheap wallpapers featuring characters from books or nursery rhymes

10. Wallpaper depicting the
Coronation of Edward VII,
c.1901–2. Machine-printed
from engraved copper rollers.
The Whitworth Art Gallery,
The University of Manchester,
W.1967.189

were being issued alongside others commemorating events such as the
coronation of Edward VII [Plate 10] and the Boer War.

In the 19th century it was often suggested by critics that consumers
who sought novelty were somehow deficient in taste.[34] Nevertheless the
popularity of pictorial products continued unabated into the 20th
century, and in the post-Second World War period, as austerity receded
in the UK and elsewhere in Europe and more people decorated their
own homes and travelled abroad, wallpapers patterned with everyday
objects or depicting leisure activities were produced in large quantities.
These papers illustrated characters from popular literature, nursery
rhymes and cartoons, or – often in a self-consciously 'arty' way [Plate 11]
– celebrated the consumption of leisure and consumer goods and the
interest in media celebrities.

Wallpapers depicting cultural icons, such as the Beatles or Marilyn, have
been dismissed as vehicles for promoting the latest film, fad or teen
idols. But is this all they are? It is undeniable that many wallcoverings of
this type are products of an industry that targets its audience precisely,
exploiting the demand it has created by ensuring immediate
recognition and, sometimes, identification on the part of its consumers.
If, however, we accept that 'cultural icons get enmeshed in people's
everyday lives and social relations',[35] these products can be seen to have
another dimension – providing a medium by which the largely young
female consumer, in the case of, for example, Barbie or Spice Girls
wallpaper, makes meanings that connect with her social experience and
thereby provide her with the motivation to resist the forces of
patriarchal control. But, herein lies the contradiction: although Barbie
[Plate 12] might be depicted standing alone, independent and free of
constraint, she can succeed only as long as her confident gaze at the
viewer is non-confrontational. And, despite being positioned as
proactive like Barbie, the Spice Girls subvert ideas of aggression by

turning in their toes, mimicking stereotypical 'little-girl' behaviour [Plate
13]. There is no such constraint for young male consumers, whose walls
can be papered with depictions of action-packed sports, adventures –
terrestrial and otherwise – and images of male celebrities famed for
their prowess with guns and girls. The enduring popularity of James
Bond continues, and the subject matter depicted on the Bond
wallpaper, issued in 1966 [Plate 14], remains as culturally relevant now
as it was when first printed. At a time when Pop Artists were depicting
slick nudes and pin-ups in one-off artworks, this mass-produced
wallpaper reflected for the popular market many aspects of Western
culture – male chauvinism, fetishism of guns and gadgets, xenophobia
masquerading as patriotism, and assumptions about taste and class. The
boy who likes knitting finds no place here.

What do we see when we look at these papers? Almost all so-called
novelty papers deploy images that are instantly recognizable. By
illustrating activities, and reflecting allegiances to particular sports,
groups or lifestyle aspirations, the papers are not only a celebration of
something enjoyable but also a confirmation of personal identity.
Already there is a whole generation for whom the Beatles (as much an
inspiration to young males in the 1960s as the Spice Girls were to girls in
the 1990s) are ancient history. But those for whom such figures are a part
of a personal history tend to regard them with deep affection, even as
empowering. As decorative devices, these representations are as
important as any acanthus leaf or arabesque; as symbolic devices they
are as important as any other; and it could be said that, although all
motifs are symbolic in some way, these are particularly so because a form
of contemporary narrative is being employed to decorative effect.[36]

Wallpaper pervades our lives, invades our lives. In some cases it
overwhelms us and, more often than not, by providing a decorative
distraction, it destroys our ability to recognize how our choices are

11. June Lyon, *Carafe*, mid-1950s. Hand screen-printed wallpaper. Manufactured by John Line & Sons Ltd. The Whitworth Art Gallery, The University of Manchester, W.1987.290.18. Hand-printed 'arty' papers such as this were often used throughout the interiors of new restaurants and coffee bars. In a domestic interior it would probably have been hung on one 'feature' wall.

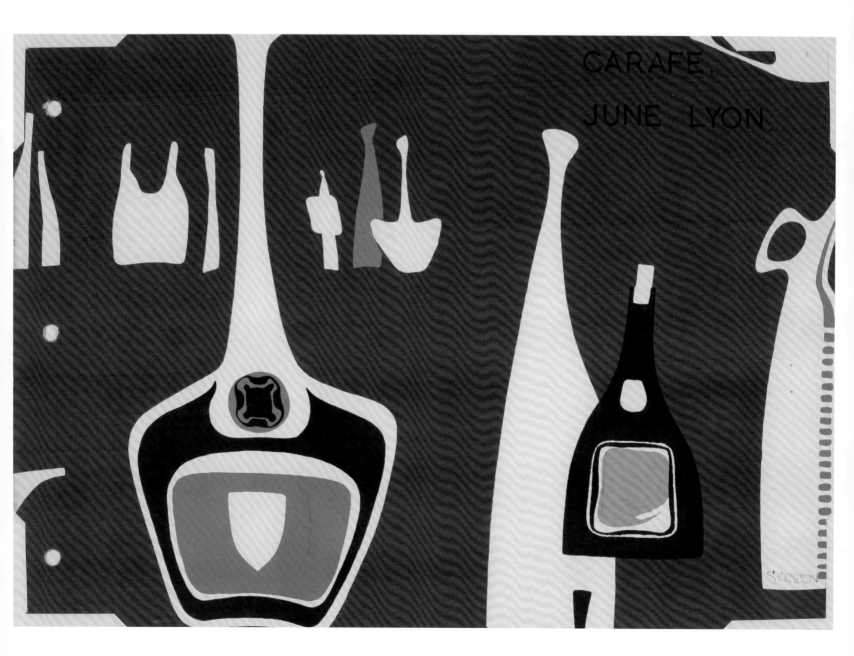

OPPOSITE:

12. *Barbie*, 1990s. Machine-printed by Vymura plc under licence from Mattel Inc. The Whitworth Art Gallery, The University of Manchester, W.1999.35

LEFT:

13. *Spice Singles*, 1997. Machine-printed by John Wilman Ltd. The Whitworth Art Gallery, The University of Manchester, W.2001.1

influenced by social and cultural norms. These norms so enmesh us that the constraints they impose are welcomed as old friends, in the same way that a prisoner might welcome a gaoler.

Papered walls have always 'talked', but the involvement of contemporary artists engages the viewer in a radically different dialogue – one that employs some aspects of the traditional visual language of wallpaper, but also uses its power to challenge, oppose and disturb. Wallpaper's perceived function is thereby subverted, causing anxiety and unease. However, in using wallpaper to reflect Western culture are artists revealing uncomfortable truths or, by repeating them, rendering them acceptable? When we view Abigail Lane's *Bloody Wallpaper* [Plate 15] the pattern of which was taken from photographs of a crime scene in the New York Police Department files,[37] are we horrified by the representation of the last desperate marks of a murdered woman or have we become desensitized to depictions of violence? Does the repeating pattern made from the bloody handprints remind us of the everyday occurrence of domestic violence or do we respond to it as an example of 'good' design? Had it been generally available when first exhibited in the 1990s it is unlikely that this work would have been commercially popular. Only a decade or so later it seems likely that, if available now, *Bloody Wallpaper*'s novelty value would earn it at least a niche market.

Repetition of floral trails and trellises allowed the Victorian consumer to bring the outside inside, to create an indoor Garden of Eden, a 'home beautiful'. But, paradoxically, their paper might have made them physically or mentally ill. Depending on the rules of the time, the hanging of particular styles of pattern displayed either the consumer's awareness of current fashionable taste or their innate vulgarity. Choosing wallpaper has always been a tricky business, and our feelings towards it have always been ambivalent. From small beginnings as a

decorative novelty for the middle and upper classes, through its controversial passage as carrier of noxious vapours and instigator of mad episodes, wallpaper has become both the silent witness of and active participant in Western culture, acting as an important social and cultural signifier. In regarding wallpaper as nothing more than 'white noise' we allow ourselves to ignore rather than address its power.[38] It is this power that has been harnessed by contemporary artists.

In the essays that follow Gill Saunders looks at the different ways in which contemporary artists have used wallpaper to explore controversial themes and discusses the influence of their work on the emergence of an interface between their art practice and that of a new breed of artist/designer-makers. Dominique Heyse-Moore shows how the domestic 'background', in the guise of educator, transformer and comforter, contributes to the reinforcing of both cultural stereotypes and patterns of social and personal behaviour. Finally, locating wallpaper in the context of the traditional view of it as the 'guilty vice of the homemaker', Trevor Keeble focuses on the work of the artist Catherine Bertola and, applying a forensic eye, suggests that wallpaper embodies the tensions created by the opposition of aesthetic experience and domestic consumption. In doing so, he concurs with the other authors in reaffirming Oscar Wilde's assertion: wallpaper is neither neutral nor particularly benign.

Christine Woods

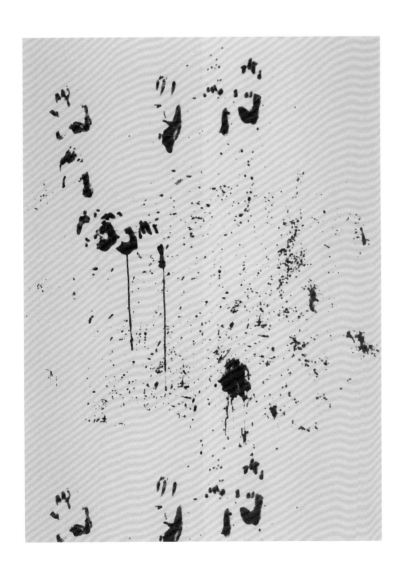

15. Abigail Lane, *Bloody Wallpaper*, 1995. Hand screen-printed wallpaper. The Whitworth Art Gallery, The University of Manchester, W.1995.13. © 2009 Abigail Lane. All rights reserved. Courtesy Karsten Schubert, London

References

1   *IKEA*® 2010 (annual catalogue), p.15.

2   Elsie de Wolfe, *The House in Good Taste* (New York: Century, 1913), p.55, quoted in Penny Sparke, 'Interior Decoration and Haute Couture', *Journal of Design History*, vol.21, no.1, 2008, p.101.

3   Anon., 'Chit Chat', *The Art-Union Monthly Journal*, vol.1, 1839, p.87. I am grateful to D. Greysmith for drawing this to my attention.

4   Walter Crane, *The Claims of Decorative Art* (London: Lawrence and Bullen, 1892), p.176, quoted in Christine Woods, '"A Marriage of Convenience": Walter Crane and the Wallpaper Industry' in *Walter Crane 1845–1915: Artist, Designer, and Socialist* edited by Greg Smith and Sarah Hyde, London: Lund Humphries, 1989, p.67.

5   See Bernard Jacqué, *Art, Progrès & Industrie: Les tableaux de papier peint* (exhibition leaflet, Rixheim: Musée du Papier Peint, 2001), p.1, and François Pupil, 'Scenic Wallpaper's Relation to the Visual Arts' in *French Scenic Wallpaper 1790–1865* edited by Odile Nouvel-Kammerer, revised edition, Paris: Flammarion, 2000, pp.136–61. In England, Metford Warner, proprietor of Jeffrey & Co., was credited with the inclusion for the first time of wallpapers in an exhibition at the Exhibition of Fine Arts at the Albert Hall in 1873: see A.V. Sugden and J.L. Edmondson, *A History of English Wallpaper 1509–1914* (London: Batsford, and New York: Scribner, 1926), p.211.

6   Linda Sandino, review of Colin Painter (editor), *Contemporary Art and the Home* (2002), *Journal of Design History*, vol.16, no.3, 2003, p.264.

7   For a survey of the involvement of artists with wallpaper in the 19th and 20th centuries, see Charles Stuckey, 'Wallpaper as Art: A Brief History' in Judith Tannenbaum and Marion Boulton Stroud, *On the Wall: Contemporary Wallpaper* (exhibition catalogue, Providence: Rhode Island School of Design Museum of Art, and Philadelphia: Fabric Workshop and Museum, 2003), pp.35–49. I am indebted to Jeremie Cerman for permission to publish his discovery of the wallpaper illustrated in Plate 2. See J. Cerman, *Le papier peint autour de 1900: usages et diffusion de l'esthétique Art nouveau en Europe dans le décor intérieur*, unpublished Ph.D. thesis, University of Paris 1 Pantheon-Sorbonne, 2009, vol.1, pp.403–404 and vol.2, pp.498–499.

8   *Moot Points: Friendly Disputes on Art and Industry between Walter Crane and Lewis F. Day* (London: Batsford, 1903), p.11.

9   René Magritte, unpublished manifesto 'L'Art pur', quoted in Marilyn Oliver Hapgood, *Wallpaper and the Artist: From Dürer to Warhol* (New York: Abbeville Press, 1992), p.187.

10 Dianne Lawrence, 'Wallcoverings: Elements of Genteel Homemaking in the British Empire', *Wallpaper History Review*, 2008, pp.47–51. This essay is based on information from 'Material Culture and the Transfer of Female Gentility to the British Empire during the Latter Half of the 19th Century', Lawrence's unpublished Ph.D. thesis, Lancaster University, 2009.

11 Jane Gordon Clark, *Wallpaper in Decoration*, New York: Watson Guptill, and London: Frances Lincoln, 2001, p.9.

12 Werner Möller, '"No Risk, No Gain": Strategies for the Bauhaus Wallpaper' in *Rasch Buch/book 1897–1997* (Bramsche: Rasch, 1998), pp.110–27.

13 G. F. Green, 'A Love Story' in *New Writing* edited by John Lehmann (London: Hogarth Press, Spring 1939), p.67. I am grateful to D. Greysmith for drawing this to my attention.

14 Leigh Hunt, *Autobiography* (3 vols, London: Smith Elder, 1850), quoted in E. A. Entwisle, *A Literary History of Wallpaper* (London: Batsford, 1960), p.71.

15 J. W. von Goethe, *Aus meinem Leben: Dichtung und Wahrheit*, 1811, quoted in E.A. Entwisle, op. cit., p.53. Entwisle lists quotations and other references to wallpaper from 1509 to 1960.

16 Richard C. Nylander, Elizabeth Redmond and Penny J. Sander (editors), *Wallpaper in New England* (Boston: Society for the Preservation of New England Antiquities, 1986), p.6.

17 Anthony Wells-Cole, *Historic Paper Hangings from Temple Newsam and Other English Houses* (Temple Newsam Country House Studies 1; Leeds: Leeds City Art Galleries, 1983), p.45. The famous Chippendale died in 1779; it was to his son, also Thomas (1749–1822), that the perplexed client wrote.

18 For wallpaper-related accounts of this period, see Joanna Banham, 'The English Response: Mechanization and Design Reform' in *The Papered Wall* edited by Lesley Hoskins (London: Thames and Hudson, and New York: Abrams, 1994), pp.132–49, and Gill Saunders, *Wallpaper in Interior Decoration* (London: V&A Publications, 2002), pp.99–109.

19 W.J. Loftie, *A Plea for Art in the House* (London: Macmillan, 1876), p.89.

20 Henry Morley, 'A House Full of Horrors', *Household Words*, 4 December 1852, quoted in Gill Saunders, op. cit., p.99; Anon., Letter to the Society of Arts, reprinted in *The House-Furnisher*, 1 April 1871, p.33.

21 Mrs Beeton, *Housewife's Treasury of Domestic Information* (London: Ward Lock, c.1865), p.211.

22 Mrs Ernest Hart (editor), *The House Beautiful and the Home*, vol.3, 1904, p.8.

23 Charlotte Perkins Gilman, *The Yellow Wallpaper and Selected Writings* (London: Virago, 2009), pp.6, 10.

24 H. A. Lediard, 'Arsenic in Domestic Fabrics', *Transactions of the Sanitary Institute of Great Britain 1882–3*, London: Offices of the Sanitary Institute, 1883, vol.4, p.112, quoted in Christine Woods, 'Delirious Fancies and Noxious Vapours: Wallpaper, the Enemy Within', unpublished conference paper delivered at *Town House Interiors & Domestic Wallpapers*, Victoria and Albert Museum, London, 10 November 2001.

25 The debate continues; see Luke Harding, 'Trousers Button up the Mystery of how Napoleon Met his Final Waterloo', *The Guardian*, 5 May 2005, and Stuart Jeffries, 'Napoleonic Wars', *The Guardian*, 16 October 2003.

26 Malcolm Morris, 'Arsenic' in *Dangerous Trades* edited by Thomas Oliver (London: Murray, 1902), p.380, quoted in Christine Woods 'Delirious Fancies', op. cit.

27 Henry Reid, *A Practical Treatise on Natural and Artificial Concrete* (London: Spon, 1879), p.335, quoted in Christine Woods, 'Delirious Fancies', op. cit.

28 Louis C. Parkes and Henry R. Kenwood, *Hygiene and Public Health* (London: H.K. Lewis, 1901), pp.250–1, quoted in Christine Woods, 'Delirious Fancies', op. cit.

29 For example, 'My wallpaper and I are fighting a duel to the death. One or the other of us has to go', quoted in *Oscar Wilde: His Life and Confessions* by Frank Harris (New York: Covici Friede, 1930), p.572, from which subsequent versions derive, such as 'My wallpaper is killing me, one of us must go', quoted in E.A. Entwisle, op. cit., p.134.

30 Letter from Charles Kean, of the Wall Paper Workers' Union, to A. V. Sugden, Chairman of the WPM Ltd., 22 January 1932, Modern Records Centre, University of Warwick Library, MSS/39/3/41/10, quoted in Christine Woods, 'Delirious Fancies', op. cit.

31 Mary Schoeser, 'Off the Shelf: Design and Consumer Trends since 1970' in *The Papered Wall* edited by Lesley Hoskins (revised edition, London: Thames and Hudson, 2005), p.237. For further information see also pp.241–7.

32 I am grateful to Frank Cockerill of Dresden Papier GmbH for this information.

33 Gill Saunders, op. cit., pp.133–6.

34 By the end of the 19th century most novelty papers were produced by the sanitary printing process. For information about the process and contemporary critical response to these products, see Christine Woods, 'Those Hideous Sanitaries: Tracing the Development of Washable Wallcoverings', *The Quarterly*, journal of the British Association of Paper Historians, no.26, April 1998, pp.1–5, and no.27, July 1998, pp.17–19.

35 Mary F. Rogers, *Barbie Culture* (London: Sage, 1999), p.6, quoted in Christine Woods, 'Sugar and Spice – and All Things Nice?', *Wallpaper History Review*, 2001, p.20.

36 Christine Woods, 'Sugar and Spice', op. cit., p.21.

37 For an image of the crime scene, see *Abigail Lane* (exhibition catalogue, London: Institute of Contemporary Arts, 1995), p.9.

38 The full quotation is 'Many people think of wallpaper as no more than white noise for the eyes – predictable, innocuous and forgettable', Julie Mehta, 'Rolling out Wallpaper: Artists are Using Off-the-wall Techniques to Design Wallpapers that Demand Attention', *Art Business News*, February 2004.

How Wallpaper Left Home
and Made an Exhibition of Itself

One of the most persistent themes in the art of the past decade has been the investigation and re-creation of domestic spaces and domestic furnishings. The essential privacy and enclosure that characterize domestic space have been disrupted or interrogated by projects that relocate the domestic in the public arena – either in galleries or in non-art spaces such as schools, warehouses, or cafes – that have been co-opted for site-specific installations. Many of these domestic dramas and explorations of home, memory and identity are played out against a backdrop of a specially designed wallpaper, which has its own part to play in the *mise en scène*.[1] Despite the critic Michael Fried's injunctions against the theatrical tendency in modern art, recent installation projects have readily embraced the theatrical and performative as they have embraced the decorative. Wallpaper has served as the scenery, providing an eloquent backdrop to the props, the 'noises off', and the actors – usually the audience themselves – who are the temporary inhabitants of these 'domestic' spaces.

But why wallpaper? With a few notable exceptions, wallpaper has mostly been the poor relation of the decorative arts, being inherently ephemeral and often overlooked: it is mostly the work of anonymous or forgotten designers, and is by its very nature intended for a role in the background rather than a place at centre stage. Indeed by the later 20th century wallpaper had become a bit of a joke, a cliché with connotations of kitsch, and as such hardly the most obvious medium for a contemporary avant-garde artist. In the context of modern art, the word 'wallpaper' has usually been employed as a term of abuse or of disapproval, to imply failure, a falling off into the vacuous or merely decorative – as when the critic Harold Rosenberg argued that the ever-larger canvases of the American Abstract Expressionist painters lacked the authenticity and challenge 'associated with risk and will' and that the result was 'apocalyptic wallpaper'.[2] In the same spirit, John Updike described a Richard Diebenkorn painting as 'an expensive variety of wallpaper',[3] and a German journalist dismissed the paintings of 2006 Turner Prize winner Tomma Abts as looking 'like pattern samples from a GDR wallpaper factory'.[4]

The word itself has become a pejorative term, used to describe anything that is bland, banal, repetitive, predictable, something that serves as background, or in the words of critic Julie Mehta, reviewing *On the Wall*,[5] as 'white noise for the eyes'.[6] And of course wallpaper is identified almost exclusively with the domestic interior, even if that domestic interior is as grand as the Lord Chancellor's apartments at the Palace of Westminster (so expensively and controversially refurbished with Pugin wallpapers in 1998). This association with the domestic was damning, for by the later 20th century the home had come to be identified with tradition, convention and conformity, and consequently domestic references had been ruthlessly excised from art galleries, both public and commercial. Galleries had become severe and comfortless 'white cubes', in marked contrast to Victorian museums and galleries, which were the equivalents of drawing rooms furnished with flock wallpaper and over-stuffed sofas. Many of these new galleries were former industrial spaces, or were styled to appear as such, often on a vast scale and with such features as poured concrete floors. In these spartan present-day exhibition spaces, wallpaper has offered a way for artists to re-connect with the domestic and also to draw on the vast reservoir of meaning, reference and association – negative and positive – that wallpaper brings with it. By producing wallpapers with their own designs or with motifs appropriated or adapted from other sources, artists have rehabilitated the domestic as a theme within avant-garde practice. At the same time they have found an effective strategy for exploring ideas about home, identity, memory and childhood, as well as engaging with aesthetic issues around the contested categories of pattern, decoration and representation.

Wallpaper has proved immensely useful in this context, because of its close, almost clichéd association with the home, and because it offers the simplest and most immediately effective way of transforming a public space so that the viewer understands it as 'domestic'. These artists' wallpapers may have motifs and designs drawn from contemporary life, they may subvert existing patterns, they may use unconventional printing techniques, but there are evident and deliberate continuities between them and historic wallcoverings, especially those of the 18th and 19th centuries, which artists draw upon for motifs or meanings, as well as for contextual resonance.

Wallpaper, as a signifier of 'home', can be powerfully evocative, triggering memories of the past, particularly memories of childhood and early life. This is vividly realized in John Smith's short film *Blight* (1994–6): as the camera pans across and around a house in the process of being demolished, it returns again and again to the wallpaper thus exposed in the upper rooms; a fragmented narrative of reminiscence in voice-over includes an elegiac refrain alternating 'I remember, I remember…', with 'I don't really remember' as former residents recall their lives in the street that was once their home. Featuring in the incantatory list of things remembered or not remembered are specific aspects of the interior decoration: the colours – 'sickly yellow', 'mushroom', 'that turkey colour', and 'the most hideous red wallpaper', as well as the 'wood chip' and 'the Lincruster [sic] wallpaper'. Wallpaper, it seems, can act upon the unconscious like Proust's madeleine, conjuring wistful elusive memories of times past.[7]

One of the defining features of wallpaper (with a few notable exceptions) is pattern, a sequence of repeated motifs. Repetition can be associated with the routine and the predictable (thus we speak of people exhibiting a 'pattern of behaviour'), but in a more pejorative sense it is associated with obsession, and with conditions such as

Obsessive Compulsive Disorder (OCD), in which simple everyday activities (such as hand-washing) are repeated to a disabling degree. The sensations and effects of repetition are the subject of a number of the wallpapers discussed here, often with specific reference to the home and to domestic life.

Pattern – and decoration generally – have since the early 20th century been consistently associated with a series of perceived negatives, notably femininity, frivolity and decadence. In a much-cited essay published in 1908, the Viennese architect Adolf Loos equated ornament with crime, permissible only to the primitive, the poor and the ignorant, and described the tendency towards decoration as a symptom of degeneracy. Indeed wallpaper is specifically implicated; Loos claims in one example that someone who can listen to the music of Beethoven [great art that has superseded ornament] but then sit down to design a wallpaper pattern must be a fraud or a degenerate.[8] Modernism eschewed ornament and argued for the stripping away of decorative embellishment, even from the domestic interior, in favour of pure unsullied functionalism. Le Corbusier, Modernism's most influential architect, conceived the house as 'a machine for living in'[9] and to that end he excised or subordinated the traditional markers of homeliness and domestic comfort. The home itself was seen by some as actively deleterious to masculine virtues; Wyndham Lewis argued that the 'alert, combative' and 'energetic' 'City man' was reduced to 'an invalid bag of mediocre nerves, a silly child' enduring a 'wretched vegetable existence' in his 'villa in the suburbs'.[10]

In this context, avant-garde artists frequently defined themselves by their antipathy to the domestic, and adopted various strategies to evade the deathly embrace of a domestic setting for their work, including vast size, industrial or ephemeral materials, and ultimately dematerialization. A shift began when Pop Art challenged the prevailing orthodoxies,

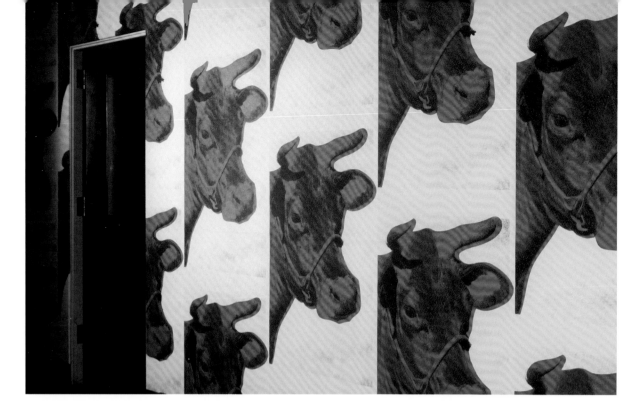

17. Andy Warhol, *Cow* [detail], 1966. Hand screen-printed wallpaper. Photo: Burstein Collection/Corbis. © The Andy Warhol Foundation for the Visual Arts/Corbis

introducing an iconography rooted in the everyday and rehabilitating the domestic as a fit subject for the fine artist. Pop's formal embrace of the domestic motif was followed by a more emotional engagement in the work of feminist artists investigating the home, and their relation to it. The expressive potential of domestic materials and motifs was a revelation. The home and its accessories have featured strongly in the art of recent decades, from Tom Wesselmann's bathrooms, Patrick Caulfield's unpeopled interiors, and Judy Chicago's *The Dinner Party* (begun 1974) to Rachel Whiteread's cause célèbre, *House* (1993), and the mutant furnishings of Mona Hatoum, Robert Gober and Doris Salcedo. However, as Christopher Reed has pointed out, these depictions of domesticity 'did not challenge conventional modes of avant-garde production (the one-off or limited edition object) and display (the museum or commercial gallery).'[11] Wallpaper, however, has allowed artists to operate outside of these constraints, producing work that has blurred the boundaries between fine art and commercial product[12] and provided the means to enact a domestic tableau in any space from boiler room and basement to washroom and warehouse.

—

Needless to say, it was Andy Warhol (1928–87, US), that connoisseur of all things kitsch and commercial, who first reinvented wallpaper as fine art. For Warhol, of course, it was the negative connotations of wallpaper that appealed – he liked the fact that it was a mass-market ephemeral commodity characterized by a repeating pattern. Producing wallpaper was an obvious choice for an artist obsessed with repetition, and with the methods and media of mass-production and the banal images of popular culture – in particular, domestic culture. Warhol was already using screen-printing to produce his paintings, and he often used the same motif over and over in series. In a 1964 exhibition he hung 28 of the small format 'Flowers' paintings in rows, completely covering a large

partition wall, creating an effect very similar to that of wallpaper or printed fabric. He described them as looking like a 'cheap awning'. Complaining that Warhol's exhibition smacked of Salvador Dali-like commercialism, the art critic Thomas Hess wrote 'It is as if Warhol got hung up on the cliché that attacks "modern art" for being like "wallpaper" and decided that wallpaper was a pretty good idea.'[13] Elsewhere, in grid compositions of motifs such as Campbell's soup cans and Coca-Cola bottles [Plate 16], Warhol was already exploring the decorative virtue of repetition. The repeated motif is transformed, rendered meaningless by the process of repetition. As Warhol said 'I like boring things. I like things to be exactly the same, over and over again.'[14] He later amplified this statement, saying 'I don't want it to be essentially the same – I want it to be exactly the same. Because the more you look at the same exact thing, the more the meaning goes away, and the better and emptier you feel.' In his search for this lack of affect, wallpaper was simply the next logical step, and he produced his first – *Cow* – in 1966 [Plate 17].

The precise origins of this wallpaper design have been lost in competing claims. The gallery owner Holly Solomon allegedly asked Warhol to design a paper as a background to the silkscreen portraits of herself that she had commissioned from him in 1966, but she baulked at the estimated $6000 production costs. Meanwhile Warhol was declaring to critic Ivan Karp that he was bankrupt of ideas, using up images too fast. Karp suggested that he 'paint some cows, they're so wonderfully pastoral and such a durable image in the history of art', to which Warhol replied 'Of course! Cows! New cows! Fresh cows!'[15] The source of the image he used for his wallpaper is uncertain; it may have come from a collection of photographs of cows, which, according to Karp, Warhol amassed in order to explore the motif's potential. Some say it was adapted from the picture on a milk carton. The most striking thing about this prosaic found image is that it is completely unsuitable for a wallpaper: the motifs do not interlock with each other across adjoining

18. Andy Warhol, *Mao* [detail], 1974. Hand screen-printed wallpaper. Photo: Philippe Caron/Sygma/Corbis. © The Andy Warhol Foundation for the Visual Arts/Corbis

sheets. As a simple unintegrated repeat that gives the illusion of three-dimensional cows' heads obtruding from the wall, printed in acid Pop colours – pink on a yellow ground, later yellow on blue – *Cow* resembles a printed filmstrip for a motionless movie (Warhol was of course a film-maker too, subverting that genre by producing films that were sequences of still images or unmoving figures). The *Cow* wallpaper was printed by Bill Miller's Wallpaper Studio, New York, in an unlimited edition, but with 100 pieces signed by the artist (nowadays these regularly come up in the sale rooms, as single images, framed like prints). It made its first appearance in one room of Warhol's show at the Leo Castelli Gallery, April–May 1966.

Warhol exhibited his wallpapers in galleries, sometimes with paintings hung against them – as with his first showing of the *Mao* paper (portrait heads of Chinese leader Mao Zedong on a white ground) [Plates 18 and 19] in Paris in 1974, which he described as creating the feel of a comfortable salon – but they were not used to create explicitly 'domestic' spaces. Warhol's *Mao* paper looks back to an earlier wallpaper style – specifically the 18th century 'Print Room'-style wallpapers [Plate 20], which were themselves *trompe l'oeil* simulations of a contemporary fashion for pasting cut-out prints on walls, with the addition of printed paper frames, swags and garlands to complete the decorative scheme. The *Mao* wallpaper belongs to a series of Warhol works inspired by Richard Nixon's 1972 visit to China, and in this application of topical subject matter to a wallpaper pattern Warhol again had an earlier precedent: many of the despised pictorial papers of the 19th century [Plate 21] illustrated – or commemorated – newsworthy events such as military victories or Royal anniversaries, or cultural events such as the opening of the Great Exhibition of 1851. The wallpaper also of course mirrors the proliferation of portraits of Mao in China itself, where every public and private building was obliged to display his likeness. Warhol's installation on the one hand asserts the redundancy of the repeated image, but at the same time recognizes its power as a tool of propaganda and social control, and as a means of producing homogeneity and conformity in society. This repeated image represents a kind of visual brain-washing, like the endless repetition of slogans from Mao's ubiquitous 'little red book'.

Warhol exploited wallpaper for its banality and everyday-ness; he was not specifically concerned with its domestic connotations, and his installations did not employ wallpaper as a means of 'domesticating' the gallery space. However, many of the artists who have since chosen to design wallpapers for installation projects have done so precisely in order to reference the domestic interior, and the experiences of domestic life.

The American artist Robert Gober (born 1954, US) has designed several wallpapers for installations, and, like Warhol, he has used 'found' images as the basis for his designs, but in Gober's case these have been used in conjunction with other objects and with domestic furnishings to build narratives around racism, sexuality, and gender politics. Gober's earliest sculptures were dollshouse-sized miniatures [Plate 22], for which he also designed wallpapers with motifs – repeated glimpses of a highway, horse-drawn wagons – that speak of an urge to get away, to escape a destiny shaped and confined by the home, and by childhood experience. He then moved on to staging full-size domestic interiors furnished with miscellaneous props including mutant objects and truncated bodies. The dollshouse of course, can be closed and secret, or open and public, and the lives within can be manipulated by a child imitating and acting out adult behaviours and relationships. In Freudian theory the survival of the home as an institution for socialization depends on the repression of fear and desire, with carnal urges relegated to the recesses of the unconscious. As Nancy Spector has noted, in Gober's art the phenomenon of repression is evoked through allusion to the body, and to the house in which the body is contained

19. Installation view of
*Le Grande Monde d'Andy
Warhol* showing *Mao*
wallpaper, Grand Palais, Paris,
2009. Photo: Benoit Tessier/
Reuters/Corbis. © The Andy
Warhol Foundation for the
Visual Arts/Corbis

and restrained.[16] The house and its furnishings become analogues for the human body, just as Freud believed that dream images of the house and its attributes represent, albeit in veiled form, libidinal impulses and individual body parts.[17]

Wallpapers have been an essential part of Gober's installations first and foremost because of the way they act as a convenient shorthand to describe 'home'. He has described his installations as 'dioramas about human beings seen from one perspective,'[18] suggesting a pseudo-scientific anthropological presentation of human lives in a domestic context, viewed as if on stage. (Dioramas, now largely discredited as fantasies projecting the mores of their times, were once popular features of natural history museums, where they were commonly used for presenting the appearance, familial relations and lifestyles of early hominids, as well as birds and animals.)[19] Gober has also stressed the importance of wallpaper itself as his chosen medium, noting that critics often engaged with the imagery without addressing the implications of his use of wallpaper. In fact wallpaper's role in enveloping the room, making 'an enclosure' with a distinct domestic resonance, was central to his purpose.[20] But by designing wallpapers in which conventional decorative motifs are replaced by subtly provocative or obliquely disturbing imagery, Gober also draws attention to the ways in which social, sexual and political attitudes and codes of behaviour become ingrained by a process of repetition and familiarization so insidious and stealthy that we neither notice nor question them. These attitudes are derived from home, family, friends and school – the sum of influences and environments that constitute what we call our background – and wallpaper often serves as the literal background to the events and relationships of our early life and development.

Certainly for the Victorians this link between the decoration of the home and the character of the child growing up in it had been explicit. They

23. Nursery wallpaper illustrating episodes from the book *Robinson Crusoe* by Daniel Defoe, English, *c.*1875–1900. Machine-printed from engraved metal rollers. V&A: Museum no. E.714-1952. Given by Mr Wyndham Payne. © V&A Images/Victoria and Albert Museum, London

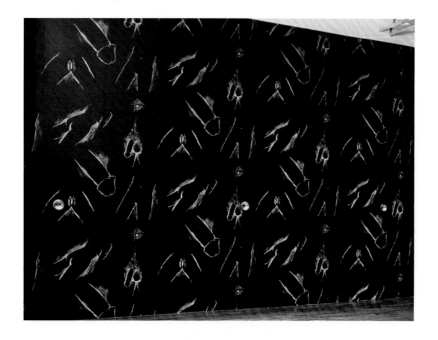

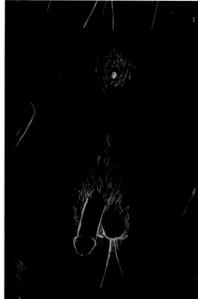

saw the home as the source of a child's moral education, and the mother – the 'angel in the house' – as responsible both for teaching the child *and* for decorating the home in such a way as to reinforce her lessons. The 19th-century literature on home decorating told its readers that the furnishings of the home were vital tools for imparting sound moral values to children. Those furnishings that '[taught] a lie' – by, for example, allowing illusionistic decoration to violate a flat surface, such as a wall – exercised a 'bad and prejudicial influence on the younger members of the house, who are thus brought up to see no wrong in the shams and deceits which are continually before them.'[21] To this end women were urged to choose wallpapers that were 'chaste' and 'honest' – in other words, wallpapers that were simple in design and true to their two-dimensional character. Overt moral messages were often found in the design of nursery wallpapers: for example, scenes from *Robinson Crusoe* [Plate 23] encouraged the white middle-class child to recognize in himself an innate superiority to the savage and 'primitive' peoples of the British colonies, and fostered his aspirations to courage and leadership.[22] A paper with scenes from *The Pilgrim's Progress* offered other improving examples to its infant audience. For little girls, exemplary acts of charity and kindness were to be found in designs by Kate Greenaway and others.

Robert Gober uses wallpapers to symbolize the way these moral influences pervade the home and childhood experience. For example, with *Male and Female Genital Wallpaper* (1989) [Plates 24 and 25], with its sketchy awkward drawings, he brings the childish scatological graffiti from the walls of the public lavatory into the home, and in doing so makes a comment on the secrecy and privacy that surround sexual identity and sexual experience, especially within the family. The genitalia images had their origins in the artist/writer publishing programme at the Whitney Museum, New York. Gober worked with a story by Joyce Carol Oates, and the genital images were intended for

the endpapers of a limited edition book. The problems Gober encountered in getting the Whitney to print these images were part of the impetus behind his idea to enlarge them for wallpaper.[23] At the same time, by applying this design to wallpaper he suggests our irrepressible curiosity about sex, which is pictured all around us in contemporary life – in advertising, in films and TV, in the press and now on the Internet. This public openness is contrasted with the situation in the home, where sex is often a difficult, or taboo, subject, a source of embarrassment and shame for parents and children alike. Gober also intended this wallpaper as an oblique commentary on the AIDS epidemic, at its height in the US in the late 1980s and early 1990s, when this paper was first made and exhibited. By making a public display of what is conventionally hidden, private, or even shameful, he shows that one consequence of the AIDS crisis was that sexual practices became the subject of unprecedented public discourse, debate and education, but also led to discrimination targeting gay men. In some versions of this installation the papered walls were pierced at intervals with stainless-steel sink drains, in an obvious further reference to social and cultural inhibitions around bodily fluids and waste matter, and to domestic rituals addressing contamination and cleanliness. Gober's wallpaper, along with his distorted furnishings such as *Tilted Playpen* (1986), might be seen as a riposte to the conservative promotion of 'family values' in this period, when the Republican administration and the media were repeatedly labelling those with HIV and AIDS as 'perverted' and 'unnatural', and, by implication, as threats to that conservative shibboleth, the nuclear family.[24]

Gober further explored the idea that we are shaped by our background and social context in another wallpaper, also designed in 1989; *Hanging Man/Sleeping Man* [Plates 26 and 27], printed in sugary colours, juxtaposes images of a sleeping white man and a black man who has been lynched. The sleeping man came from a newspaper ad for

Bloomingdale's bed linen, the hanged man from a political cartoon published in Texas in the late 1920s (found in the picture collection of the New York Public Library).[25] Gober has said that this juxtaposition was intended to implicate the white man in this peculiarly American crime. As he saw it, this 'was an image of troubled sleep, a dream of something horrible that had happened, but it was also multi-layered, there was a piece missing in that puzzle about the crime, about what happened and what the story was, and it was left up to the viewer. It was a Rorschach kind of image. Also the sleeping man could have been dreaming, so there was the possibility that this was a racist fantasy or dream.'[26]

We might also see it as suggesting complicity, if not direct guilt; turning a blind eye to distressing or unpleasant things, letting them fade into the background of our lives as we do the wars, crimes and injustices we see daily on our TV screens and in our newspapers, but feel powerless to affect. And in the relentless repetition there is the recognition that history repeats itself, that these crimes were replicated all across the Southern states, and that they have continued in the regular demonization of and discrimination against black Americans. Around the time that Gober's exhibition with this wallpaper opened in Washington, DC, the city's black mayor, Marion Barry, who had recently been accused of drug offences, claimed that he had been the victim of entrapment, and he was quoted on the cover of the *Washington Post* saying 'I was lynched.'[27] In another high profile case soon after, the black judge Clarence Thomas, newly appointed to the Supreme Court, referred to the sexual harassment suit brought against him by his former colleague Anita Hill as 'a high-tech lynching for uppity blacks.'[28]

Gober was aware that by translating such imagery into the 'pretty pattern' of a wallpaper he was reinforcing its offensiveness, but by taking wallpaper as his medium for this particular message, he underscored an unpalatable truth – that racism (and demonization of

the 'other' (which, for Gober, included gay men, another beleaguered minority subject to blatant discrimination) is routine, a constant refrain running through our lives, whether black or white. Gober suggests that whites are unthinkingly guilty of racism, and that blacks see racist attitudes everywhere, justifiably or not. This became apparent when the paper was shown as part of Gober's collaboration with Sherrie Levine at the Hirschhorn Museum, Washington, in 1990. Gober was surprised – perhaps naively – when African American employees at the museum found the imagery to be racist and offensive, and refused to accept his assurances that he meant well in his use of such motifs. It was by no means clear to them that his intention was to call into question an unthinking acceptance of racist views, and not uncritically to represent or even to reinforce such views. Entrenched positions on either side – the white liberal sure of his own good intentions and politically correct stance, and the black museum staff, seeing only racial slur and insult – were an ironic enactment of the theme of the wallpaper design. Indeed, as Gober later surmised, the use of wallpaper – a 'debased medium' – compounded the offence by seeming to trivialize a profound and hurtful subject.

Gober has repeatedly returned to wallpaper as the medium that best expresses the power of home and family to affect the character and psyche of the child. For *Forest* (1991) [Plate 28] he drew directly on common childhood influences – picture books and fairy tales. The design was adapted from a textbook illustration of a deciduous forest, but Gober imbued this innocent motif with a powerful sense of menace and unease. The forest is often the place where the significant action of a fairy tale takes place; it is a place of danger and of encounters with dark forces. It is where Hansel and Gretel are abandoned and meet the witch, and where Little Red Riding Hood encounters the wolf. As Bruno Bettleheim has written, 'the near-impenetrable forest in which we get lost has symbolized the dark, hidden near-impenetrable world of our

28. Robert Gober. *Forest*,
1991. Hand screen-printed
wallpaper. Installation view,
Galerie Nationale du Jeu de
Paume, Paris, 1991. Visible:
Forest, 1991, *Cigar*, 1991,
Untitled, 1991 and *Untitled*,
1990. Photo: K. Ignatiadis/
© Courtesy of the artist

unconscious.'[29] Elsewhere in literature the forest is characterized as a place of danger, but also of discovery and transformation.

Gober's wallpaper forest, with its reversed and inverted perspectives, is literally a 'world turned upside down', disrupting the sense of order and security we expect to find in the home. The effect is remarkably similar to the kind of Piranesian fantasy that was created in domestic interiors by the use of the so-called 'pillar and arch' wallpapers of the later 18th century. This style of paper is characterized by impossible multiple vanishing points that induce a vertiginous sense of disorientation in the viewer. The repeated verticals and blank vistas are oppressive and, like Gober's *Forest*, they create a sensation of being imprisoned. This sense of enclosure that the viewer experiences with *Forest* is not unlike that created by certain 19th-century French scenic decorations, but where the wooded landscape of *Chasse de Compiègne* (1812) offers glimpses of open country, and the rampant flora of *L'Éden* (1861) or *Le Brésil* (1862) [Plate 29] suggest the lush abundance of a nurturing paradise, *Forest*, with its bar-like vertical trunks and autumnal colouring, evokes a more malign environment. Stepping into a room decorated with this paper is to enter a Freudian landscape of hysterical projection and fearful hallucination. But a more optimistic interpretation is also possible: though we may feel we are trapped in an identity forged in childhood, the home can also serve as a space for the imagination, an arena in which we learn to become adults and from which we set out on new paths.

—

A number of artists have used 'found' patterns, taking existing designs from wallpaper or textiles, as the basis for their own wallpapers. Some modify their found designs, interpolating new motifs; others simply rescale, or re-present the pattern they have appropriated, relying on a new context to supply the meaning. One who has taken the former

approach is the African American artist Renée Green (born 1959, US). Using the visual language of domestic decoration she has explored black history, and the way it is misrepresented through a selective preservation (and presentation) of objects and images from the past. *Commemorative Toile* [Plates 30 and 31] is a pattern she produced as wallpaper and fabric for an installation called *Taste Venue*, first shown in New York in 1994. At first sight it appears to be a direct reproduction of the 18th-century copper-plate-printed cotton textiles known as toiles de Jouy (so-called after the French town where they were first produced).

Green's design conforms to the characteristic style of the original textiles, printed in a single colour on white with finely detailed picturesque scenery, decorative elements, and detached figure subjects framed by flora and fauna. But she draws not only on the decorative tradition of toiles de Jouy and their English counterparts, she also adopts the convention of producing such textiles with patterns that make reference to historical events, including political subjects. An historical example of this is a toile made around 1792 depicting scenes from the French Revolution [Plate 32]. Indeed when one looks more closely at the detail of Green's design one sees that the conventional scenes of amorous couples are interspersed with discordant images of violence, and with black characters as well as white, in scenes taken from a number of 18th- and 19th-century engravings.[30] In one vignette a Haitian revolutionary lynches a white French soldier, and in another we see the Senegalese heroine of an early 19th-century novel *Ourika*, who was cast out by her French benefactors for the crime of falling in love with the son and heir. Other scenes include a slave market and illustrations to texts recording the abolition of slavery.

Green uses this wallpaper design to make some complex and serious points about history. She suggests that those artefacts that have

LEFT:

30. Renée Green in collaboration with The Fabric Workshop and Museum, *Mise-en-Scène: Commemorative Toile*, 1992. Installation at The Power Plant, Toronto, 1998. Hand screen-print on paper-backed cotton sateen wallpaper, and hand screen-print on cotton sateen upholstered furniture. Photo: Will Brown/© Courtesy of The Fabric Workshop and Museum and the artist

BELOW:

31. Renée Green in collaboration with The Fabric Workshop and Museum, *Commemorative Toile* [detail], 1992. Hand screen-printed on paper-backed cotton sateen. © Courtesy of the artist and Free Agent Media

32. Valance in toile de Jouy fabric showing scenes from the French Revolution, French, c.1792. Plate-printed cotton. Designed by Jean-Baptiste Huet. V&A: Museum no. 1682–1899. © V&A Images/Victoria and Albert Museum, London

OVERLEAF

LEFT:

33. Carrie Mae Weems, *Looking High and Low*, from the 'Africa Series', 1993. Hand screen-printed wallpaper. V&A: Museum no. E.262-2000. Given by the artist. © V&A Images/Victoria and Albert Museum, London

RIGHT:

34. Zineb Sedira, *Une Génération de Femmes*, 1997. Hand screen-printed wallpaper. Produced at The London Printworks Trust. The Whitworth Art Gallery, The University of Manchester, W.1999.15. © Courtesy the artist and Galerie Kamel Mennour, Paris

survived into the present – and especially those that are preserved and displayed in museums and thus given special status as historical evidence – show us only one highly selective version of history, a history that is largely – often exclusively – one of white wealth and success. She hints that much of this wealth was built on black labour, including slave labour (the cotton trade in the southern US was founded on black slave labour). But Green's design balances this by warning against a simplistic revisionist view of history by deliberately choosing imagery that reminds us that Africans in the 18th century were not simply victims or chattels – many were educated, independent and fully capable of self-determination.

Like Robert Gober, Green uses furnishings to show how beliefs, behaviours and perceptions are woven into the fabric of daily life. Both use pattern, with its predictable structure of order and repetition, to represent familiar ideas and received wisdom, and both subvert it by incorporating imagery that is 'out of context' and acts to disrupt expectations and comfortable assumptions.

Carrie Mae Weems (born 1953, US) also appropriated an existing pattern for a wallpaper she made as part of a larger installation, *The Apple of Adam's Eye,* at the Philadelphia Fabric Workshop Museum in 1993. Called *Looking High and Low* [Plate 33] it is directly recycled from a woodcut design by the English illustrator John Farleigh for the endpapers of George Bernard Shaw's story *The Adventures of the Black Girl in Her Search for God*, first published in 1932. Weems felt that this small-scale repeat, almost abstract its graphic economy, was an apt backdrop for a photographic record of her own spiritual odyssey to the slave ports of West Africa. As she put it in an interview with curator Thomas Collins, 'I was a subject in search of myself and attempting to map a new psychological terrain for myself and others. I suppose […] I'm trying to construct a new prism for looking at certain aspects of African American

culture.' As she says, 'the wallpaper is a metaphor for the searching, probing, looking.'[31] Weems's taking-back of a white artist's 'Africanizing' design in this context highlights the historic European appropriation of Africa, its people, culture and resources – her own heritage.

The French artist Zineb Sedira (born 1963, France; lives in the UK) was also drawn to making wallpaper because it offered the opportunity to use the structure of repeating pattern as a medium to question cultural stereotyping. She produced a repeat grid pattern as a wallpaper and, in a variant version, as ceramic tiles, for her degree show at the Slade School of Art, London, in 1997. The wallpaper is entitled *Une Génération de Femmes* [A Generation of Women] [Plate 34] – the women in question are the artist herself, her daughter, her mother and her grandmother, whose faces can been seen faintly printed in red 'behind' the grid. Sedira is French, but born of Algerian parents, so it is apt that she took a conventional Islamic pattern as the basis for her design. Traditionally, Islamic art did not permit the representation of living things, but Sedira has subverted this male-dominated artistic tradition by introducing the female figure. So she connects with and draws upon her own cultural heritage, while at the same time asserting her own identity as a Westernized woman artist. She has said that she also intended the design to be a criticism of Western concepts of Islam, which have often assumed that Islamic patterns are purely decorative – in fact she says these patterns employ a sophisticated geometry 'permeated with symbolic, cosmological and philosophic significance'.[32] The faces here look out from the gaps in the grid like women segregated from male company behind pierced screens, as they are in traditional Muslim households. The grid pattern is crisp, but the faces are blurred. Nevertheless, these women's faces, repeated over and over, are an integral part of the pattern as a whole – and thus Sedira reminds us that women, even if they are confined to the home, and segregated within it, are integral to social and to familial structures. Though they

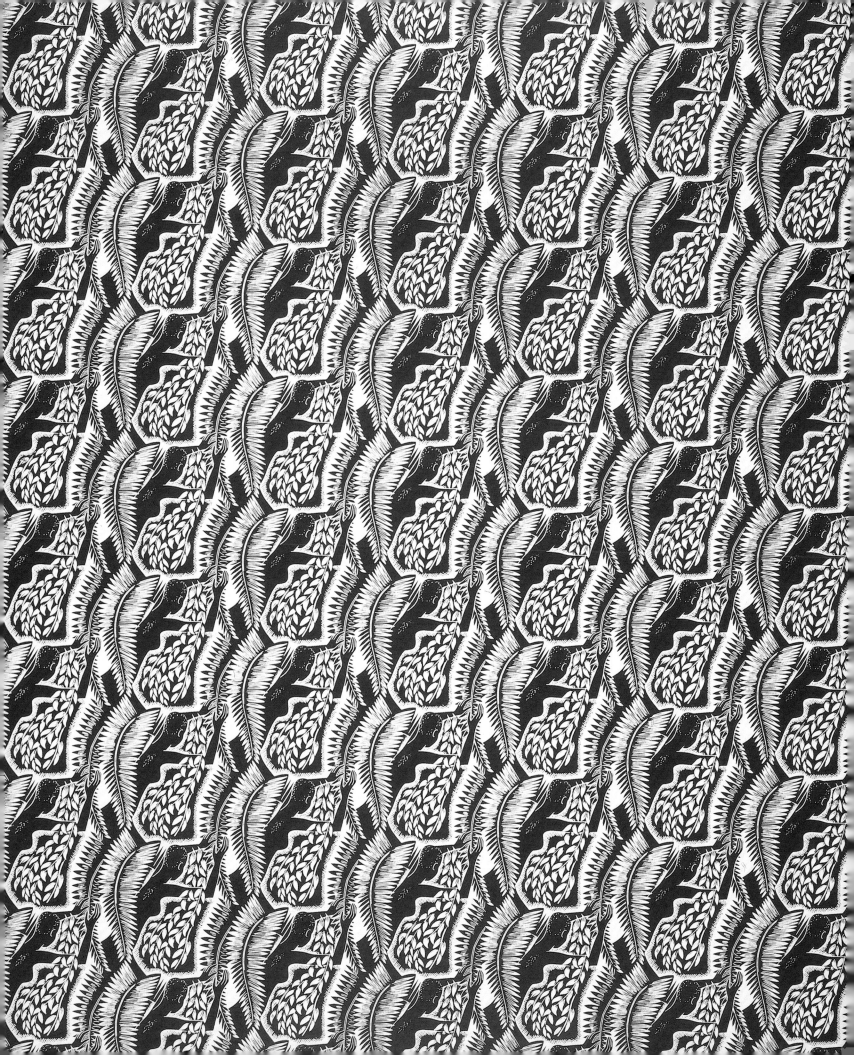

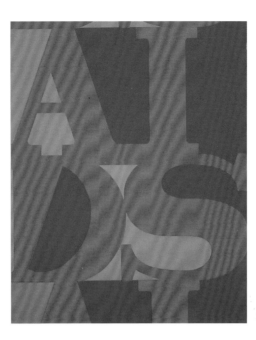

might be individually constrained, together they support and strengthen the institutions of which they are a part, just as the use of a consistent pattern in construction – building or weaving, for example – confers strength, protecting against collapse or unravelling. The title also plays on the meanings of the word 'generation': to generate is to reproduce, to reproduce is to repeat. In this way, Sedira implies that patterns of behaviour, attitude and belief may be repeated in succeeding generations, becoming literally enmeshed in the fabric of home and family.

This strategy of disrupting or subverting patterns has been employed for more explicitly political and propagandist ends as well as for exploring personal histories. In the late 1980s the Canadian artists' collective General Idea designed a wallpaper that was based on Robert Indiana's famous *Love* painting from 1966 [Plate 35] (later editioned as a screenprint in 1967) but with the letters L.O.V.E replaced by A.I.D.S. [Plates 36 and 37] General Idea used this logo to promote AIDS-awareness in public places and they printed it on carrier bags and posters as well as on wallpaper. It has been exhibited in many museums and galleries. The adaptation of Indiana's LOVE motif implies a causal link between the sexual liberation of the 1960s and the sexually-transmitted illness that surfaced in the 1980s. One four-letter word replaces another, love mutates into illness and death. The image also gives us a graphic metaphor for the action of the HIV virus itself – the LOVE motif has been 'infected' and has mutated from something benign to something dangerous: like the cells invaded by HIV it has kept its form but changed its nature. And by repeating the motif in a wallpaper pattern the artists hint that we might see it as imitating the replication of the HIV virus in the host cells.

But General Idea also intended something more positive when they reproduced this stark acronym as a wallpaper pattern. At the time they produced this image, there was widespread ignorance and prejudice surrounding AIDS; phrases such as 'gay plague' were used in the media in a way that implied that those who contracted AIDS were being punished for adopting 'deviant' lifestyles. General Idea wanted to counteract the prevailing tendency either to ignore or to demonize those with HIV or AIDS. Their avowed intention was simply to normalize the disease as an illness, and not a stigmatizing self-inflicted punishment. Also, by adapting the motif to everyday familiar situations, using homely materials such as wallpaper, they confronted the shame and secrecy imposed on people with AIDS and reminded us that most continue to live ordinary domestic lives. At the same time, the wallpaper hints at the house-bound routines that a debilitating illness imposes on sufferers: before retroviral drugs controlled the effects of the disease, people with AIDS were often confined at home, with no life outside their own four walls.

Francesco Simeti (born 1968, Italy, lives in the US) has exploited wallpaper as a medium for explicit political commentary and protest, as well as a means of creating what he describes as 'hidden narratives'.[33] Most of his papers are responses to site-specific commissions; others have been prompted by compelling found images. Simeti has designed patterns with motifs such as military helicopters, parachutes and exploding bombs, but he has also used digital media and photomontage techniques to modify several historic wallpaper patterns, subverting decorative designs by inserting images culled from newspapers showing scenes of combat and conflict, and their consequences. In one of his first, *Acorn* wallpaper (2001) [Plates 38 and 39], Simeti took the decorative frame motifs from an 18th-century 'Print Room' paper[34] [Plate 20] but substituted the fêtes galantes of the original with scenes showing figures in bio-hazard suits moving toxic waste. In *Arabian Nights* (2003) [Plates 40 and 41], a pattern by Jean-Baptiste Réveillon from 1789, showing a manicured park landscape with lakes, decorative bridges and pergolas, is

37. General Idea, *AIDS*, 1988. Acrylic on canvas. *AIDS Wallpaper*, 1989. Hand screen-printed wallpaper. Installation view, Württembergischer Kunstverein Stuttgart, 1992. Photo: Courtesy the Artist

40. Francesco Simeti,
Arabian Nights [detail], 2003.
© Courtesy of the Artist and
Francesca Minini Gallery,
Milano

peopled with Afghan refugees toting their belongings by donkey and bicycle, and doing their laundry in the lake waters. *Clearing Fields* (2001) [Plate 42] has a similar landscape, copied from a monochrome toile pattern and printed to resemble grainy magnified newsprint, to which Simeti has added photographic images of soldiers in Northern Ireland and Kosovo (both civil wars driven by ethnic enmities). The soldiers are 'clearing fields', in the sense that they are clearing minefields, but are also following the imperatives of 'ethnic cleansing'. Just as Martha Rosler did in her seminal photomontage series *Bringing the War Home* (about the Vietnam War), Simeti brings warfare (here the conflicts in Iraq and Afghanistan) into the domestic arena. But where Rosler showed battles raging outside suburban picture windows or erupting into living rooms, Simeti blends his imagery seamlessly into wallpaper patterns – an explicit demonstration of how we have become inured to such scenes on our TV screens, and allow them to fade into the background. There is also the suggestion here that these 'colonial' wars being fought in the Middle East and Afghanistan (for control of oil and other commodities, and avowedly to protect the West from terrorism) underpin the successful economies – and thus the comfortable lifestyles and luxuriously appointed homes – in the West.

Another artist who has brought the realties of war into the domestic context with a powerful graphic immediacy is Bashir Makhoul (Palestinian born 1963, Israel; lives in the UK). His *Points of View* wallpaper (1998) [Plate 43] shows repeated details of plastered walls pock-marked with bullet holes (derived from photographs taken in Beirut). The wallpaper design, narrowly focused on these details, avoids the specificity of time or place, becoming (like Simeti's papers) a comment on the way in which distant wars and hatreds are undifferentiated background noise unless or until they impinge directly on our own lives. But because Makhoul is a Palestinian, we also read his wallpaper as a dramatization of a particular conflict; with this simple

bullet-hole motif, Makhoul confronts us with the fundamental crisis of daily life for Palestinians in Gaza and the Occupied Territories (and for many in Lebanon too). Their homes do not offer the certainty of safety or security; they are fragile, and as vulnerable as the lives of their occupants.[35] Home – in the sense of a domestic family dwelling, but also a place of national identity, and belonging (home-land) – is an ideal that is repeatedly fractured by hostility, violence and exile. Instead of

43. LEFT: Bashir Makhoul, *Points of View*, 1998. Installation at Bluecoat, Liverpool, UK, 1999. © Courtesy of the artist. OPPOSITE: *Points of View* [detail], 1998. Machine-printed from flexographic rollers. Design and roller preparation by 3D Decorative Designs Ltd., printed by A.L. Wallcoverings. The Whitworth Art Gallery, The University of Manchester, W.1998.5. © Bashir Makhoul

'papering over the cracks', and disguising the realities of the Palestinians' plight, Makhoul uses wallpaper to make their circumstances explicit, reminding us that Palestinian homes have been repeatedly bombed or bulldozed, literally invaded by violence, their inhabitants living as refugees in their own lands.

Violence as a fact of daily life, but embedded in a culture of religious belief, is also the subject of the *Wounds* wallpaper [Plate 44] of Conrad Atkinson (born 1940, UK; lives in the US). This is one of a series of works made since 2003 in which Atkinson has abstracted 'the wounds of Christ' from medieval and Renaissance paintings of the Crucifixion and the Pièta (in the collections of the Metropolitan Museum, New York, and the Courtauld Institute, London). These motifs retain their original identity, but are shown to connect to more contemporary events, such as the AIDS crisis and the political history of Northern Ireland. Atkinson has engaged repeatedly, over a long career, with the Northern Ireland 'Troubles', and has also made a wallpaper showing the laughing faces of Martin McGuinness and the Rev. Ian Paisley, once implacable enemies, but latterly colleagues as leading members of the Northern Ireland Assembly, following the rapprochement achieved in 1998 by the Good Friday agreement. The *Wounds* wallpaper can be read as a reference to the religion that each side – Catholic and Protestant – has invoked to define their tribal identity and thereby justify their murderous attacks on their neighbours. Much as Abigail Lane does with her *Bloody Wallpaper*, Atkinson has translated graphic emblems of Northern Ireland's sectarian violence – a long saga of feuding with killings and bloody retributions – into a seemingly neutral pattern. But here the use of pattern underscores the repetitive nature of the events: an eye for an eye as each faction responds to one murder with another, the hatred becoming integral to the lives of successive generations. Indeed children were often witnesses to the violent death of a parent or brother, since a favourite strategy was to kill victims on their own doorsteps, a strategy that contributed to a

rigid segregation of the opposing communities, living parallel lives on either side of defensive walls.

—

Though it is so often overlooked, wallpaper occupies a position of intimacy in our lives and it can express significant aspects of the character of the home and of its inhabitants. The choice of a wallpaper can reveal – or at least imply – much about class and economic status, as well as alluding more discreetly to sexual, political and moral orientations. Thus wallpaper can be readily co-opted by the artist to any attempt to explore the relationship between ourselves and the spaces we live in. It has long been believed that homes express the personalities of those who live in them – or are designed to project a particular image of the inhabitants. The home itself constitutes a personal narrative of aspiration, taste, social status and identity, as well as serving to frame familial and other proximate relationships. We see our homes, and the way we choose to decorate them, as having an influence on our characters and on our behaviour: colours can affect our moods; patterns can either agitate or intrigue; small rooms can be experienced as cosy or claustrophobic, depending on one's point of view. Spartan interiors are thought to toughen people up, whereas soft and comfortable furnishings may well seduce us into self-indulgent sedentary lifestyles.

These ideas have their origins in the 19th century, and much decorating advice of the time stressed the importance of using furnishings to create a calm and harmonious home, as a sanctuary from the pressures of the outside world. The choice of wallpaper was seen as a key component in this enterprise – soothing unassertive designs characterized by 'soft and gentle harmonies…and a small pattern' were regularly recommended in home-decorating manuals of the period.

One such guide – Mrs Beeton's *The Housewife's Treasury of Domestic Information* (1865) – advised that in the choice of wallpaper for a bedroom '… care should be taken…to avoid any outré forms which the eye of a restless invalid, condemned to many hours of solitude, could torture into a form or a face of demon or grotesque horror.'[36] Robert Edis warned against 'strongly-marked patterns', which could be 'a source of infinite torture and annoyance in times of sickness and sleeplessness', with 'a ghastly and nightmarish effect upon the brain.'[37]

In his *Bullies* wallpaper [Plates 45 and 46] Virgil Marti (born 1962, US) deliberately flouted these rules to create a pattern that represents the manifestation of projected fears. The looming faces in the pattern are taken from the photographs of boys in Marti's junior high school yearbook, forbiddingly titled *The Padlock*. These are the nightmare visions of a bullied adolescent, perhaps the faces of the tormentors encountered daily by Marti himself as a gay teenager in a world of assertive heterosexuality in which 'jocks' and tough guys were predominant. The wallpaper itself is a fluorescent flock that can be seen to full effect only in a darkened room under blacklights. As we know, darkness tends to magnify anxieties that are suppressed, or moderated, by day – just as the fluorescent colours give an intimidating emphasis here to images that, if seen by daylight, would be no more than a pattern on paper. Most of us will, at some time, have lain awake in the dark, apprehensive or fearful of something or someone, with our minds exaggerating the threat. We have all imagined monsters in the innocent patterns of a wallpaper, a curtain, or a carpet – an experience that is often exacerbated by illness, insomnia or anxiety. This phenomenon is memorably evoked by Charlotte Perkins Gilman in her story 'The Yellow Wallpaper', in which the narrator's claustrophobia and descent into hysteria are charted through her deteriorating 'relationship' with the wallpaper in her bedroom. Describing this paper she dwells on its 'repellent… smouldering unclean' colour and its design, in which she

sees strangled heads and 'bulbous eyes.'[38] It is this kind of claustrophobic terror that Marti's seemingly innocent design conjures up – the exaggerations that an oppressed mind is subject to are mirrored in the way that the pattern takes on its intimidating emphasis only in the dark.

The basic elements of Marti's design were copied from a French toile wallpaper, to which he applied flock (chopped wool or silk, or in this instance rayon, which is glued to selected areas of the pattern to give a raised velvety pile). Since the 18th century French wallpapers and furnishings have generally represented elegance, fashion and refined taste, especially in America, where they have often been considered superior to those imported from England [Plate 47]. Flock paper was also a luxury product designed specifically to imitate the look and feel of cut velvet. By integrating these portraits of aggressive adolescent males (aptly described as 'mug shots'[39]) with the elegant lines of a French wallpaper, Marti suggests that brutality and stereotypical male behaviour coexist with, and are perhaps even nurtured by, the ostensibly superior values of the middle-class home and a 'civilized' society. Here, then, masculine forces are seen to invade the home, a space that is generally identified with the feminine. In this context they threaten to overwhelm the delicate feminine fabric of order, taste and civility.

In a more light-hearted spirit Marti has explored this clash of cultures – high versus low, feminine versus masculine – in his *Beer Can Library* wallpaper (1997) [Plate 48]. When it was first shown in the US, it was hung in a grandly proportioned wood-panelled 19th-century interior, accessorized with dark and heavy period furniture – a room with the style and scale of the library that was usually to be found in any grand and wealthy house of the period.[40] The *Beer Can Library* paper is a complete catalogue of the collection of 800 beer cans that Marti

amassed in his early teens. On the one hand it is a pun on the collecting and classifying instincts to which so many people succumb, whether the collection is of rare books, butterflies or beer mats, but we might also see it as a pop culture riff on the expensive *trompe l'oeil* wallpapers that are printed with images of book spines on library shelves. Such papers are often used in stately homes to disguise cupboards or doors in book-lined rooms.

Describing the furnishing of a room is a device often used by writers to establish the scene of a narrative, or to evoke the character of a place. A typical example of this strategy occurs in Chapter 3 of Guy de Maupassant's novel *Bel-Ami* (1885). He swiftly sets the scene, and tells us something of the life and circumstances of his amoral hero in a brief description of the wallpaper in his lodgings: 'The wallpaper, grey, with blue posies, had as many stains as flowers, stains ancient and suspicious which defied analysis, crushed remains of insects, drops of oil, smudges of fingers greasy with pomade, splashes of soap-suds from the wash

hand basin.'[41] This, the author shows us, is the squalid and impoverished reality behind the protagonist's suave public manner.

As this passage suggests, wallpaper is a silent witness to the secrets of domestic life. Our homes and our furnishings are marked with the traces of our physical presence; sagging mattresses, indented cushions, worn carpets, faded wallpapers, and finger-prints on doors and walls, are the forensic evidence of our daily domestic routines. The artist Abigail Lane (born 1967, UK) has used wallpaper to investigate her interest in these bodily traces, and to explore the transforming effects of repetition and reproduction.

Lane's first wallpaper was made in 1992 for an installation she called *Making History*[42] [Plate 49]. In this show she explored the nature of the repeated mark, and played with perceptions of authenticity. For example, she made printing blocks exactly replicating the sole of a foot or the palm of a hand; by so doing she questioned the 'truthfulness' of a

OPPOSITE:
50. Sonia Boyce, *Lover's Rock* [detail from one of a suite of 6 drops], 1998. Blind embossed wallpaper. Produced by Early Press, London, on paper supplied by Sanderson plc. V&A: Museum no. E.468-1999. © V&A Images/Sonia Boyce

footprint or a fingerprint as a proof of identity. The apparent uniqueness of our body parts is immediately subverted by the possibility of their reproduction and repetition. The wallpaper from this show comprises a series of curvaceous shadowy shapes like Rorschach blots, repeated single file down each sheet of paper. The paper was originally exhibited with a single clue to the identity of this mysterious motif – a chair with an ink pad in place of the seat – which points to the true nature of the mark: it is in fact a print of a female bottom. The wallpaper was made by alternately sitting on the chair and then on the paper. Each impression is thus unique, unlike conventional wallpaper, where each 'repeat' is mechanically printed and identical. The paper stands for all the various physical traces we leave printed or impressed on the things we live with.

But Lane is also interested in the autographic gesture, specifically the artist's touch, the imprint of the artist's hand as evidence of authenticity and value: with the *Bottom* wallpaper she mocks such pomposity, by employing a more vulgar body part to create art. She also offers a sly dig at the French artist Yves Klein (1928–62) who famously made paintings by smearing paint on the bodies of naked women, and then directed them to press their bodies against canvases, leaving an imprint of their thighs and torsos. Klein's paintings were made in the course of public performances; Lane's wallpaper, with its modest domestic associations, suggests a more private and intimate arena.

In her second paper, Lane pursued this exploration of the autographic mark, but in a darker domestic context. For an installation entitled *Skin of the Teeth*, first shown in London in 1995, she designed a wallpaper that, at first sight, appears to be a delicate crimson-on-cream abstract pattern [Plate 15]. The original exhibition included a series of clues: a giant red inkpad, a model of an expectant dog, a severed head and arms modelled in wax, and unsettling 'noises off'. As one stood in the room, these elements gradually coalesced into the evidence of a murder

scene. It was then that the wallpaper pattern revealed itself as a series of repeated hand-prints interspersed with odd trickles and splotches. The colour of course was that of blood. The exhibition notes confirmed that these marks had been reproduced by Lane from a New York Police Department scene-of-crime photograph: they represent the last desperate gestures of a murder victim imprinted on the walls of an apartment. The bloody handprints are the ultimate autographic gesture, yet in Lane's version they are replicated to the point of anonymity, emptied of their immediacy and authenticity. By repeating the marks, Lane transforms this horrific graphic evidence into the blank anonymity of a decorative pattern. But like those psychological puzzles that can be read as vases or faces, the pattern fluctuates between these two readings. In *Bloody Wallpaper* Lane is also making an oblique reference to the way in which violence can be a part of domestic life. We commonly refer to violence within families as 'domestic' violence, as if it somehow has a different character, less threatening and less dangerous than the kind that takes place between strangers on the streets – as if, in fact, it were tamed and normalized in the home, 'domesticated' by its context, and just another part of the pattern of daily life.

Lover's Rock (1998) [Plate 50], designed by Sonia Boyce (born 1962, UK), was inspired by popular music, but like Lane's papers, it represents our physical interaction with the spaces we live in. The paper is white; the only decorations are the words at about hip-height that have been blind-embossed (printed or stamped into the paper, without using any pigment, to produce a pattern in relief) on each length of paper. These words come from Susan Cadogan's hit 'Hurt so Good' (1975) – apparently this was particularly popular at West Indian house parties in the 1970s. Boyce recalls going to parties where, when this song was played, couples would rub and sway up against the walls, responding to the intense sensual message of the music. Afterwards, the wallpaper would be rubbed and marked at hip height all round the room. The *Lover's Rock*

paper is intended both to evoke and to commemorate this tactile encounter between bodies and walls and the fugitive traces left behind.

Music is also the subject of Boyce's recent *Devotional Wallpaper* (2008), generated by a larger project, the *Devotional Series*, which had its origins in reminiscence sessions at which a group of women (with Boyce herself) pooled their memories of black British musicians and singers. The result is a collective map of iconic performers. Boyce has represented these reminiscences in various ways, including an etching for the Rivington Place portfolio (2007), by inscribing the names on the walls of the National Portrait Gallery (2007), and now as silk-screened wallpaper [Plate 51], where 200 names are listed, each framed by radiating concentric lines. This roll-call of fame is also a memorial, a list of luminaries of the kind found in town halls, schools and sports clubs where the names of dignitaries, benefactors or prizewinners are recorded in solemn chronological sequence. Wallpaper, of course, lends itself rather well to this list format, but in the context of Boyce's project the paper is also a recognition of the place of popular music in our lives – as the background to dating and dancing, weddings and funerals, but also as an accompaniment to everyday routine: housework is carried out to a refrain from the radio, the CD player or the iPod.

The repeated routines of housework were harnessed by Catherine Bertola (born 1976, UK) for her contribution to the Victoria and Albert Museum exhibition *Out of the Ordinary: Spectacular Craft* in 2007–8. Bertola found a perverse inspiration in the clichéd perception of a museum as a place of musty basements in which countless treasures are entombed, gathering dust as they decay unseen. As she has done in a number of previous installations, she took wallpaper as her starting point, working with it here to uncover a hidden aspect of the V&A's history. Having discovered that William Morris's *Marigold* (1875) wallpaper once hung in the galleries, she decided to recreate the pattern in an unconventional fashion, using dust and debris gathered daily by the museum's cleaners in galleries and stores, and by the conservators cleaning and conserving the objects themselves. She then applied this ephemeral detritus to the surface of cut-paper patterns.

Bertola's cut-out version of *Marigold* [Plates 52 and 53] was 'flocked' with dust and sweepings, and the furred contents of the vacuum cleaner bag, and embellished with the desiccated bodies of moths and beetles, spiders and flies. She built the pattern week by week; adding a new branch, a new cluster of flowers, as she received the latest accumulations of dust, posted to her studio in Newcastle. By choosing

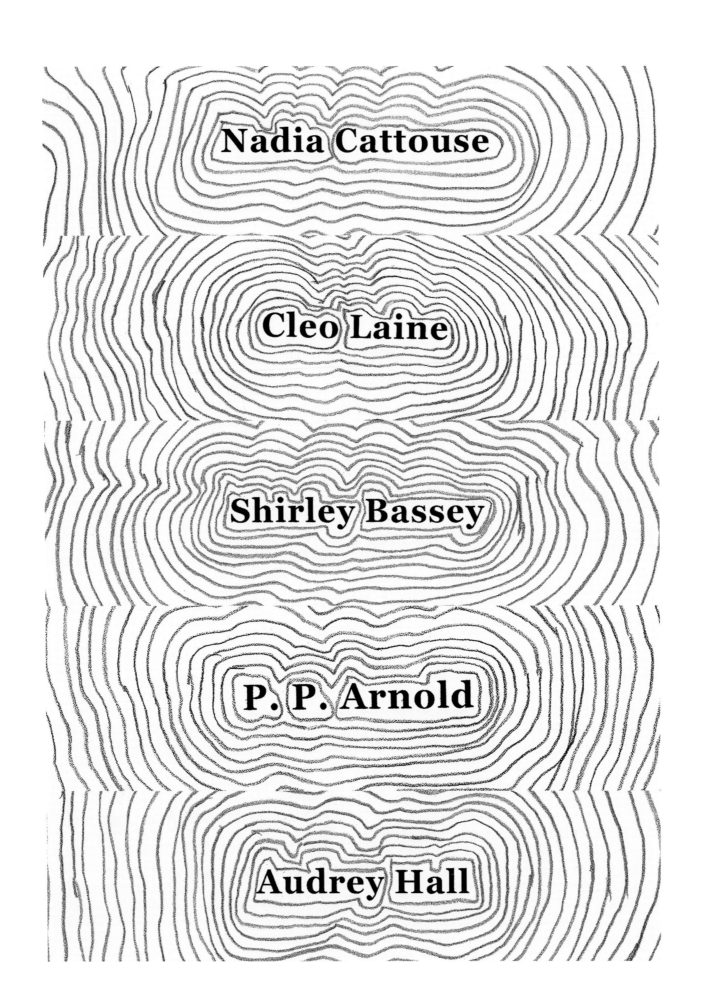

Nadia Cattouse

Cleo Laine

Shirley Bassey

P. P. Arnold

Audrey Hall

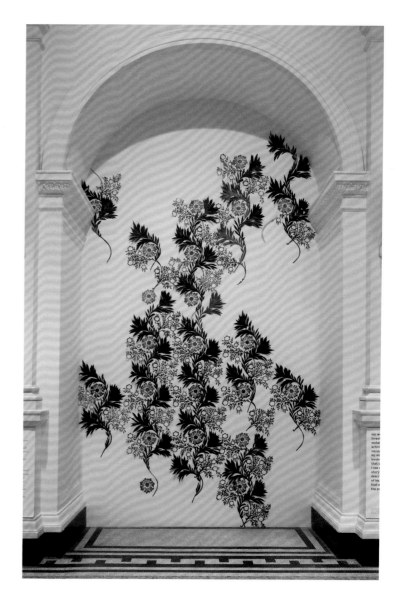

to build her installation over the course of the exhibition, Bertola made explicit the idea of the work growing out of a process of repetition – regular dusting, sweeping, vacuuming, polishing – that harvested her raw material and fed the growth of each frond and flower, the work spreading across and up the wall piece by piece, imitating the natural habits of branching and flowering. As in nature, the products of decay acted to fertilize a new creation. Indeed the paper pieces, curling and lifting from the wall, adding shadows to the dust-coloured leaves, seemed to be caught in the act of coming to life.

The installation engaged subtly with these ideas of repetition – of a decorative pattern (the wallpaper), and of a process (cleaning) – and demonstrated that even the most routine and invisible work has a part to play in the life of a museum (as also in the home), and makes a vital contribution to those more visible fruits of labour, the exhibitions and gallery displays. Cleaning is but one strand in the process of re-generation that is essential if a museum is not to succumb to the organic processes that would ultimately reduce everything to dust. In Bertola's clever metaphor, the unseen and the worthless were retrieved and revivified, their inherent redundancy briefly postponed, the shadow of history invested with fugitive substance.

—

Wallpaper has long been credited with the power to create an atmosphere of homeliness, though this effect might be only temporary or illusory. In 1813 the writer Leigh Hunt was imprisoned for libel against the Prince Regent, and he later described how he transformed his cell: 'I papered the walls with a trellis of roses; I had the ceiling coloured with clouds and sky; the barred windows I screened with Venetian blinds…Charles Lamb declared there was no other such room, except in a fairy tale.'[43] Artists have exploited this capacity, often

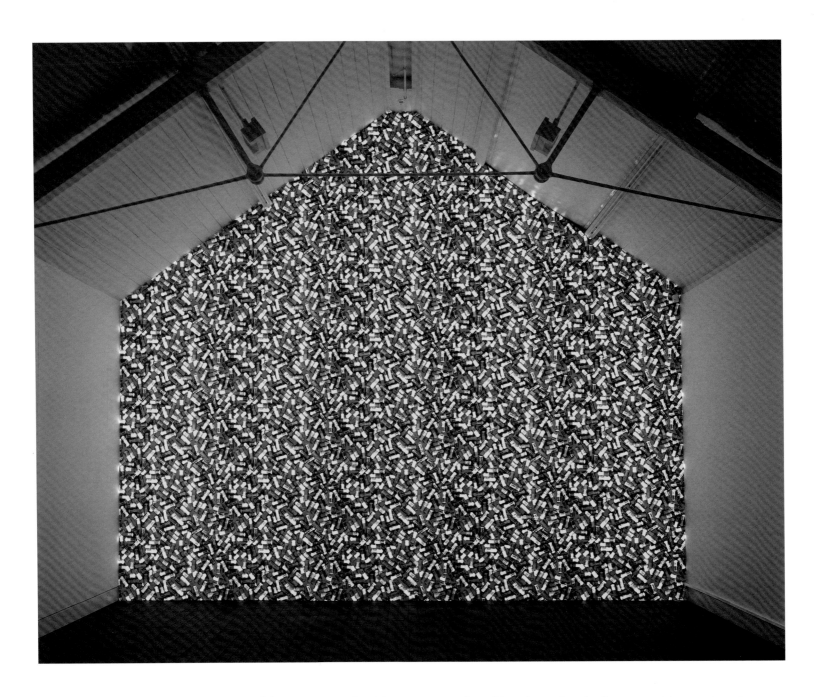

choosing to use wallpaper to give a veneer of domesticity to industrial and other large-scale exhibition spaces, or to spaces with some other defined function. At the Jerwood Gallery, for example, Virgil Marti's fluorescent *Pills* wallpaper [Plate 54] was pasted onto a full-height wall and shaped like a gable-end to reinforce further the domestic reference.[44]

Tense, an installation by Anya Gallaccio (born 1963, UK), which featured in the East Country Yard Show (1990), curated by Henry Bond and Sarah Lucas in an empty warehouse at Surrey Docks, London, included a wallpaper [Plate 55] as part of a strategy to create a domestic arena in the vast open-plan space.[45] Gallaccio has described how she 'tends to respond very formally to a space, often using the grid and repetition.'[46] The paper, printed with over-sized orange motifs,

mirrored an oblong 'carpet' on the floor comprising one ton of Valencia oranges that gradually decayed over the three-week duration of the show. The Surrey Docks area was once known as 'the larder of London' because of the amount of imported produce stored there. Gallaccio has often used natural materials – such as flowers, fruit and ice – as her raw materials, to create temporary 'paintings' and sculptures in which the process of deterioration and decay is an integral part of the work. Wallpaper too is often considered ephemeral; once hung it fades, and will become stained and dirty, may peel or buckle; eventually it will be stripped off, or pasted over and obliterated. And, like Gallaccio, wallpaper designers have often looked to nature for their motifs – most famously William Morris, whose characteristic patterns are dense with flowers, foliage and fruits (including imported exotics such as pomegranates – and oranges).

The grid and repetition are also explored in the work of Rosemarie Trockel (born 1952, Germany). Through such means as her famous knitted pictures and her 'social sculptures' she has also explored gender issues in art history, often parodying both the methods and materials of Minimalist and Conceptual art. For her exhibition *Bodies of Work* at the Whitechapel Gallery, London in 1998–9 she designed a poster/ wallpaper which was used as the backdrop to related exhibits in a space called the 'Egg Room'. The image on the wallpaper is a photograph of a section of a sculptural work by Trockel, *Egg Curtain*, 1998, which consisted of chains of blown egg-shells threaded together and suspended like a beaded curtain. This was intended in part as a nod to the egg-shell 'paintings' by the Italian Conceptual artist Piero Manzoni (1933–63), but it was also designed as an organic, 'feminine' and domestic parody of the rigid formality, grid-like structure and heavy industrial materials which characterized much Minimalist sculpture. Indeed each sheet of paper is square – a deliberate reference to the Minimalist square and cube – and when the paper is hung, the motifs do not join seamlessly from one sheet to the next. Rather the pattern is cut off at the edges in a way that implies a narrow gap between each sheet and its neighbours, thus producing a grid-like format on the wall.

The use of wallpaper as part of an exhibition space and designed both to connote domesticity and to pull together disparate exhibits has become a useful strategy for artists. In 1994 Sonia Boyce designed her first wallpaper, *Clapping* [Plate 56], for *Wish You Were Here*, an installation of domestic-style spaces created by the artists' group BANK. (In this installation it was shown in an orange and white colourway; there is also a black and white version.) The paper supplied a unifying element that also emphasized the room-set layout of the exhibition; though the muted colourway was self-effacing, the motif gave the pattern an assertive quality. The giant clapping hands appeared to applaud the works of art in the room, but also to address the viewers as they became, by default, the performers in the sequence of 'stage-set' spaces. Addressing the occupant of the room directly, the paper suggests that life is a continuous performance, a series of repeated acts, even in private. Indeed the paper is printed in oblong frames like a giant filmstrip, and Boyce has said that she was inspired by the Judy Garland film *A Star is Born*, with its theme of the self as public performance focused on intervals of applause.

In-A-Gadda-Da-Vida, a group show of mixed media work at Tate Britain in 2004 featuring Sarah Lucas (born 1962, UK), Damien Hirst (born 1965, UK) and Angus Fairhurst (1966–2008, UK), used wallpapers specially designed for the occasion by the exhibitors. The show's theme was the Garden of Eden – but this was paradise seen from a somewhat jaundiced perspective: the wallpapers both evoked the natural world, albeit a natural world owing more to genetic modification than to nature, but also brought a decorative domestic element to the high-ceilinged gallery space. Hirst's design was a vivid mosaic of butterfly wings and Fairhurst designed a multi-layered woodland pattern, distorted and out-of-focus, called *Underdone/ Overdone* (based on paintings of the same title) [Plate 57]; this looked like a landscape irradiated by a nuclear explosion, a post-apocalyptic take on the 19th-century panoramic landscape wallpapers, and their lush exotic views.

Sarah Lucas enlarged pizza delivery leaflets for her *Pizza Wallpaper*. She had previously designed a paper for her solo exhibition, *The Fag Show*, at Sadie Coles HQ in 2000. As the title suggests, the show's dominant motif was the cigarette: an eccentric collection of objects – including garden gnomes, chairs and vacuum cleaners, each with some kind of crudely jokey sexual appendage – had been covered with a 'skin' of cigarettes. These disparate objects huddled together like members of some dysfunctional family, against the backdrop of a wallpaper that

56. Sonia Boyce, *Clapping*, 1994. Hand screen-printed at The London Printworks Trust. © Sonia Boyce

57. Angus Fairhurst, *Underdone/Overdone*, Digitally printed wallpaper. Installation view, *In-A-Gadda-Da-Vida*, Tate Britain, London, 2004. © the artist/Courtesy Sadie Coles HQ, London/Tate, London

Lucas had titled *Tits in Space* [Plate 58]. This paper, with its pattern of paired spherical shapes sculpted from cigarettes printed on a matt-black ground, held the group together. The result was both visually dramatic and also very funny, suggesting the extent to which smoking is an obsessive and deeply-ingrained habit that permeates skin, clothes and furnishings, but is also a pleasure associated with everyday activities from gardening to sex. In an interview with James Putnam[47], Lucas acknowledged the 'obsessive activity' involved in making the exhibits, and described the resulting forms as 'incredibly busy […] a bit like sperm or genes under the microscope.'

The wallpapers of Michael Craig-Martin (born 1941, Ireland) present us with 'the heroics of the ordinary';[48] they show outsize isometric images of everyday objects, drawn from his database of some 200 motifs that he reproduces in various formats – paintings, prints, light boxes – as well as wallpaper [Plate 59]. Many of these motifs first appeared in his 'Wall Drawings', begun in the late 1970s and made with self-adhesive black tape. These things are ubiquitous in daily life, they 'loom large', but are so familiar that we no longer really see them, though we are dependent on their functions and they in turn are integrated into our routines, and rich in potential associations. Each of these objects and utensils – the desk chair, the book, the mobile phone, the filing cabinet, the light bulb, the soft drinks can, the fork – represent a repeated act, an everyday activity, mundane, familiar, essential. These are the pared-down motifs of a modern still life: the accessories to work (in the office, in the studio) and the daily rituals of washing, eating, relaxing. The inclusion of the classic porcelain urinal is surely a gentle nod to Marcel Duchamp's *Fountain*, that iconic work of art which freed the artist to take whatever he chose from the world of things around him. The drinking glass is perhaps a reference to Craig-Martin's own Duchampian homage, *An Oak Tree* (1973), which comprised a glass of water on a shelf.

A precursor of the now ubiquitous fashion for using wallpaper to give a domestic ambience to bars, clubs and gastro-pubs, Damien Hirst designed a wallpaper for his Notting Hill restaurant venture, Pharmacy, in 1998. Taking the contents of his drug cabinets and pill paintings as his motifs, he produced a pictorial pharmacopeia for the walls, the preciousness of the jewel-like capsules and shiny blister-packs enhanced by the gold and silver grounds. Hirst's paper acknowledges the addictive – and repetitive – aspect of drug-taking, whether those drugs are medicinal, nutritional or recreational. In the context of the restaurant, the wallpaper also (like his 'Last Supper' prints) implied that most food, the product of industrialized processes, is stuffed with chemical compounds – from artificial colours and flavours to antibiotics and growth hormones. The pills and the medicines are captioned with Biblical incidents, from miracles to damnations: Christ's assertion 'I am the bread of life' is countered in the implacable repeat by the reiteration of plagues and afflictions, and ultimately, Death. Despite our faith in modern medicines, Hirst implies that the rituals of pill-popping, like the rituals of worship, cannot not save us.

—

Artists are often attracted to wallpaper because it allows them to create large-scale work that completely envelops and transforms a space. Virgil Marti has said 'I like the idea of producing material that can be expanded or contracted to fit a room so that the architecture becomes the frame.'[49] The domestic or decorative aspect may still be relevant, but it is the transformative effect that is paramount.

This is precisely how the German sculptor/photographer Thomas Demand (born 1964, Germany) employed wallpaper in his 2006 exhibition at the Serpentine Gallery in London. Demand was prompted to design and use wallpaper as the backdrop to his photographs at this

66

particular venue by a number of factors. In the first place, he was keen to emphasize the domestic scale and the intimacy of the gallery (which was built originally as a tea-room and became a gallery only in the 1970s). The gallery's park setting was important too, and the ivy-patterned wallpaper [Plates 60 and 61] (in four colourways, ranging from the blue-black of 'Night' through the brighter greens of 'Normal' and 'Sunny' to the snow-whiteness of 'Pale') had the effect of turning the space inside out – since ivy normally grows on the outside of buildings. Though the ivy pattern appeared to be relatively naturalistic, it was actually derived from the paper cut-out leaves illustrated in one of Demand's own photographs – *Klause 2/Tavern 2* (2006) [Plate 62]. At first sight Demand's photographs appear to be records of real places, but in fact his practice involves the painstaking construction of life-size models of real places, using only commercially available paper and card; his sources are images in books, postcards and the media. This particular tavern, represented in a series of Demand's photographs, was notorious as the site of the abduction and murder of a child. In this context the ivy that fills most of the picture frame and almost obscures the blank-looking windows, conjures up fairy-tale associations of menace and danger – the story of Hansel and Gretel, abandoned in the forest by their wicked stepmother, and almost fatally seduced by the apparent sanctuary of the witch's gingerbread house, comes to mind. The encroaching ivy also suggests concealment and the covering-up of what goes on 'behind closed doors' within the family (the abusers of the child in this case included his mother and stepsister). Thus the wallpaper (in this room he hung the colourway he called 'Normal'), reproducing the dense all-enveloping ivy in the picture, had the effect of creating a sinister and claustrophobic atmosphere. Other rooms, hung with different colourways, had a correspondingly lighter mood.

Demand has been described as an illusionist for the way in which he can so convincingly transform paper and card and persuade us to see

them as constituent elements of a substantial reality – a seemingly solid world of stone, plaster, metal, wood and fabric 'built' from the most fragile and ephemeral of materials. But, of course, wallpaper has been in the business of producing illusions ever since it was invented, designed to fake the appearance of more costly materials such as wood panelling, plasterwork, tapestry and velvet, and, with the advances of printing and reproductive technologies, to imitate silks and lace, marble, tile and brick. Wallpaper's ability to trick the eye made it an obvious addition to Demand's repertoire.

The artist Richard Woods (born 1966, UK) has also made wallcoverings, though in his case these are more substantial than paper, and often applied to the *outside* of a building. Indeed his installations delight in disrupting expectations of inside and outside, and reference wallpaper's long history of imitation, *trompe l'oeil* and fakery. In *Nice Life*, at Art Basel Miami (2003), he dressed up a warehouse in a super-sized toile pattern, printed (as is all his work) on thin sheets of MDF (Medium Density Fibreboard; themselves printed from giant MDF woodblocks carved with a router). For *NewBuild*, at New College Oxford in 2005 [Plate 63], he disguised the 14th-century stone-built Long Room with a brash 'red brick'-printed cladding.[50] Red brick, conventionally a homely building material, is considered honest and unpretentious; it stands for a sturdy functional vernacular, as well as the mellow warmth associated with comfort and security. Yet the 'red brick' here had no substance, it was a flimsy sham – makeshift modernization concealing the solid centuries-old stone.

Woods's rebranded exteriors apply a clichéd homeliness to disparate buildings, but over-bright and over-sized, they announce their 'pretend' character in the 'look at me' disguise of pantomime, rather than the self-effacing disguise that aims to avoid detection. As in *NewBuild*, the scale and colour have the effect of unsettling viewers, prompting questions

capacity for imitation and pretence can easily shade into dishonesty and deceit. Wallpaper, with its facility for tricking the eye into seeing stone or brick, lace or toile de Jouy where there is only printed paper, has often been used as a metaphor for moral shallowness, or the rejection of solid traditional values. Nineteenth-century fiction abounds in such references. In one of the most telling, in Thomas Hardy's *Far from the Madding Crowd*, Sergeant Troy, handsome, flashy, and vain, is newly married to Bathsheba Everdene and thus in possession of her home, Weatherbury Farm House; he immediately expresses his discomfort, declaring 'I feel like new wine in an old bottle here.'[52] He suggests refurbishments such as stripping out the fine old oak panelling to put up wallpaper; by this proposed exchange of sham for substance, he exposes his own lack of integrity.

Lisa Hecht (born 1972, Canada) has employed wallpaper in several installations, with the intention of changing the physical and psychological perceptions of a space. These wallpapers often explore the relationship between interior and exterior, sometimes exploiting the dramatic potential of bringing outdoor motifs into a 'domestic' context. Hecht created wallpaper with the simple repeat pattern of a chain-link fence – the urban counterpart to the ivy-covered trellis pattern so popular in 19th-century wallpaper design – for an installation called *Space Contains No Threats*, first exhibited in 2000 [Plate 64]. Chain-link fences are conventionally used for demarcating boundaries and defining spaces, to contain or to exclude. The title seems ironic: the viewer in a room lined with this paper is contained – imprisoned – behind the wire, with a view of nothing but blank blue sky. In the original installation, there were strategically placed ladders that led nowhere, simultaneously offering and frustrating the prospect of escape – but also perhaps a reference to the commonplace description of someone stressed by confinement or anxiety as 'climbing the walls'. The idea that wallpaper should offer the illusion of a seductive view – as the

about the solidity and veracity of the built environment as a whole. Woods has said that his work has 'neither style nor substance',[51] a tongue-in-cheek disclaimer that takes us to the heart of his purpose. His rebranded spaces highlight the strategies many of us adopt to represent ourselves to the world, each of us putting on 'a front', an optimistic veneer that may be no more than a skin-thin bravado. In this respect Woods is exploiting to the full wallpaper's gift for 'faking it', but this

65. Kelly Mark, *12345*, 1999–2000. Hand screen-printed wallpaper. © Kelly Mark

19th-century French panoramic papers did with their scenes of the elegant streets of Paris or Rome, or exotic tropical landscapes – is drastically subverted here. The view is one of blank nowhere-ville, and the wallpaper is no longer a decorative background but a confining screen that the artist herself has described as 'camouflage'.[53]

This idea of the domestic interior as a prison has also been explored by a number of artists including Kelly Mark (born 1967, Canada), whose *12345* wallpaper (1999–2000) [Plate 65] has a pattern made from endless rows of 'five-bar gates', the hand-written marks used for counting. Screen-printed from a hand-drawn original, uneven and variable as if made with different implements, the repeated lines suggest the marking of time by someone housebound, if not actually imprisoned. The paper carries overtones of claustrophobia, and offers a witty take on the constraints of repetition, a defining feature of the monotony of much domestic routine.

Matthew Meadows (born UK) explores some similar ideas in a very different way in his *Razorwire* wallpaper [Plate 66], which was inspired by his interest in adapting historic patterns and by his experience of teaching in prison. The design of this piece is a fascinating conflation of different patterns; the underlying motifs derive from 18th-century damask, and mock-flock wallpapers, as well as 19th-century floral stripes, printed in shades evocative of historic papers. 'Woven' into these patterns are stripes created by the cut-out negative silhouettes of strands of razor wire. The 'over' and 'under' layers of pattern are so subtly interlaced that it creates a kind of *trompe l'oeil* effect, so that is not clear whether the wire motif overlays the conventional pattern or is integral to it.

The traditional wallpaper patterns combined here connote domesticity, security, comfort, and also luxury (the paper is hand-printed from woodblocks), but these associations are contradicted – indeed

graphically cancelled out – by the imagery of the wire, which immediately suggests darker feelings of pain and confinement. This imagery conjures the negative obverse of homeliness – an experience of domesticity where cosiness becomes claustrophobic, and elegant surroundings are a veneer of politeness concealing or inhibiting passion and honesty. At the same time the imagery alludes to the way that prisoners use symbolic and familiar objects to create a sense of homeliness in their cells, though this is a homeliness that is constantly contradicted by the setting, with its bars, locks and wire-garlanded walls. The choice of colours also contributes to the way we read Meadows's use of pattern. The blue represents 'outside' – space, sky, freedom, hope – whereas the black (as used in his first version) seems to stand for the negative of these qualities and emotions, and embedded in the overall design, the wire motif cancels out the optimistic associations of the blue.

Nicole Eisenman (born 1965, France; lives in the US) looked to a specific historic precedent when she designed *Gray Bar Hotel* (2003) [Plate 67], a wallpaper that illustrates scenes from daily life in a women's prison. Her cartoon-style vignettes, with inset close-ups of broken chains and portraits of impassive prison guards, are set out like a comic strip. She cited 'some English nursery wallpaper from the 1800s that I liked, with repeating scenes of the four seasons.'[54] The analogies between prisons and nurseries are highlighted in 'The Yellow Wallpaper', in which the former nursery to which the narrator is confined has bars at the windows – as nurseries often did, to prevent children falling out. Indeed the nursery was designed as a place of segregation within the home, where children lived their lives separate from the adult inhabitants, with their own staff – nursemaids, governesses – as well as their own distinctive furnishings. Like children, prisoners are subject to daily routines, devised and imposed by others; prisoners' lives are characterized by repetitive timetables that follow a predictable pattern. As in Eisenman's paper, many early nursery papers feature a grid or

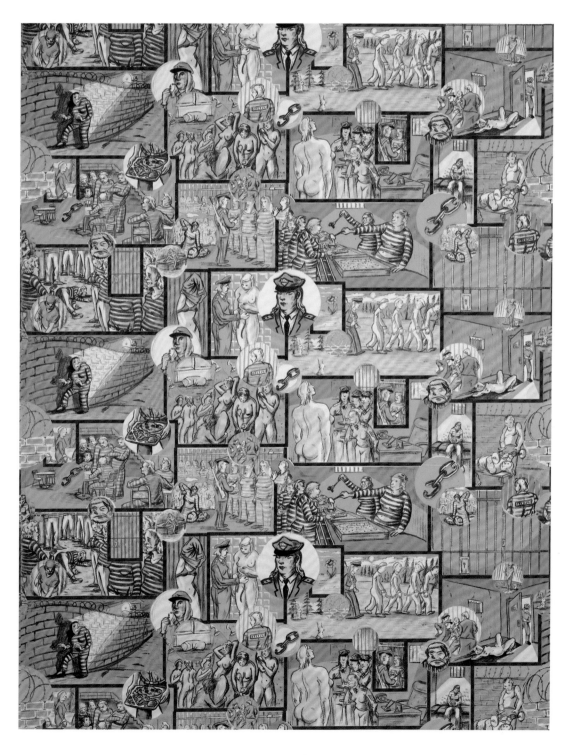

some other framing device to structure a sequential (repeated) narrative, or pictorial vignettes. A 'Four Seasons' paper (perhaps the one that inspired her) has a diamond-shaped 'masonry' lattice framing the brightly coloured scenes[55] [Plate 68], and an anonymous paper (*c.*1875–1900) illustrating episodes from *Robinson Crusoe* frames the scenes with images of driftwood or roughly hewn branches that resemble the rustic decoration of a log cabin [Plate 23].

—

Artists' wallpapers, generally speaking, are not made for commercial production or domestic use, but increasingly the ideas explored by artists making wallpapers for installations are influencing those making limited edition wallpapers and those working to commission. Just as the distinctions between art and design have been progressively blurred, so commercial wallpaper producers have increasingly co-opted the street-cred and cutting-edge kudos that come from an association with contemporary art. In consequence, materials, motifs and effects that would once have been considered inappropriate for the home are now finding a market. In 1996, Glasgow's Centre for Contemporary Arts commissioned wallpapers from four artists: David Shrigley (born 1968, UK), Adrian Wiszniewski (born 1958, UK), Hayley Tomkins (born 1971, UK) and Martin Boyce (born 1967, UK). Shrigley's design, *Industrial Estate* [Plate 69], is a cartoon vision of the anonymous uniformity of the contemporary urban landscape, with everything from carpet warehouse to garage, church and sauna inhabiting the same kind of brick box or blank-walled shed, and the same brand names appearing in every high street from Aberdeen to Penzance. It puns on wallpaper's reputation for being bland and boring, but it also takes a swipe at the increasing homogenization of our towns and cities, described in a recent report as 'cloning'. Shrigley acknowledged at the time that his wallpaper might be oppressive in the domestic interior. The same might be said of Hayley

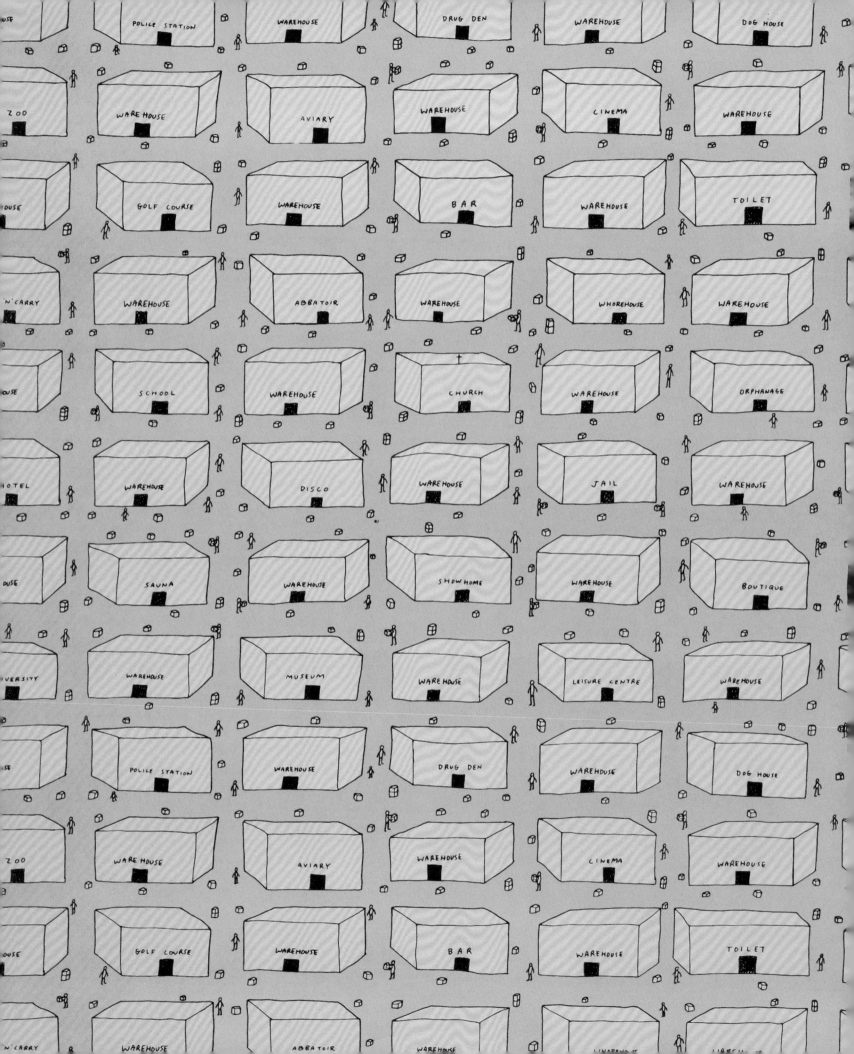

Tomkins's *Cry Baby* [Plate 70], a 'messy' design of babies' heads, many of the faces screwed up and screaming, aptly printed in shades of pink and red. Here wallpaper represents the claustrophobic dimension to family life, where the sleep-deprived parent might feel the walls closing in. These papers were commercially available, but eschewed the traditional clichés of home decorating in favour of grittier subject matter reflecting on real life, rather than the rural idyll conventionally evoked by wallpaper patterns. The papers also reflect a new willingness to introduce a self-deprecating humour into home decorating.

The designer Sharon Elphick (born 1968, UK) has also adapted a defiantly dour urban imagery to wallpaper. Inspired by her own photocollages of tower-blocks and skyscrapers, she designed *Prefab Stripe* [Plate 71] in 1998, a wallpaper printed with view of a tower block in an endless blurred repeat in dulled grainy tones. The modular units of the building ('pre-fabricated') depicted here offer a neat analogy for the 'repeat' of a typical traditional wallpaper. Though the trend towards loft living and more minimal interiors might seem to militate against the use of wallpaper, Elphick sees the shift towards large living spaces as an opportunity to use wallpaper in a new way. She believes, 'People have got the space to use an interesting paper without it dominating everything.'[56] Ironically, if hung in an urban loft apartment, her wallpaper might well mirror the views from those large windows.

Deborah Bowness (born UK) is a designer and maker of innovative bespoke wallpapers that work either as room sets or as eye-catching conversation pieces. She works to commission, using wallpaper as a way of introducing a narrative or an element of performance to a space, whether domestic, public or corporate. Bowness rarely uses repeat patterns, preferring images derived from photographs, usually her own, to create an illusionistic space that extends the walls of the room. Her characteristic method is a mix of jump-cut *trompe l'oeil* effects. The often

monochrome imagery, with pale tints or washes of colour, transforms the space, giving it a theatrical or cinematic feel. She has done a number of one-off site-specific temporary installations for public and commercial spaces, including stores such as Selfridges, Reebok and Paul Smith, as well as more permanent decorations at Soho House, a private-members' club, and Camden Brasserie, both in London.

Bowness's wallpapers can also set the scene for a personal narrative of daily life, in which real furnishings are played off against their pictorial counterparts producing a disorienting interplay between two and three dimensions. Her prizewinning *Hooks and Frocks* paper (*c.*2000) [Plate 72] is a photographic montage of dresses, chairs and bags that transforms a bedroom into a stage-set. Clients can order a personalized version featuring their own most photogenic garments, and have fun playing off the real things against their pictorial counterparts.

For an installation, *Living Rooms*, at the Museum of Domestic Design and Architecture (MoDA) in 2003 [Plate 73] Bowness devised a work of paper architecture inspired by her travels in the Far East, but rather than offering souvenir views of picturesque landscapes, she recreated the worn nondescript furnishings of a cheap hotel, the traveller's temporary 'home from home'. The wallpaper served as a collage of memories, but unlike conventional pictorial holiday mementos, it suggested that the four walls of a hotel room are more truly representative of our travels than the 'must see' sights recorded in a thousand holiday snaps. She gives us the 'anywhere' of a hotel room as the archetypal tourist experience, rather than the specificity of a teeming street, a snow-capped mountain, an ancient temple or a ruined palace. Bowness's paper is the backpacker's version of the panoramic murals that in the 19th century reproduced the cosmopolitan scenery of the Grand Tour. Here the nostalgic faded tones suggest sun-bleached settings and tired furnishings, but conjure

too the soft-focus effect of memory as the vivid immediacy of experience fades into reminiscence and anecdote.

The idea of the unique or customized decoration has been adopted for a commercial context by Chris Taylor (born 1962, UK) and Craig Wood (born 1960, UK). Their award-winning *Frames* wallpaper (for the manufacturer Graham & Brown) [Plate 74] is a modern DIY take on the 'Print Room' style. The customer can paste their own photos, drawings or magazine cuttings into the printed frames, in a more sophisticated version of a pinboard; alternatively the kids can be let loose with their felt-tips. As Craig Wood has said, the design 'plays with the taboo of graffiti and writing on the walls'[57] and offers a defined space for personal creative input into the decoration of one's own home. Taylor and Wood have revisited this idea in other projects. For the V&A's summer exhibition, *The Other Flower Show* (2004), they customized a garden shed [Plate 75] with wallpaper that had a child-like 'hand-drawn' floral pattern pasted over every surface including windows, ceiling and the back of the door. Crayons were provided for visitors to transform this black and white outline design into the 'riot of colour' so beloved of British gardeners. Running out of space to express themselves, or perhaps frustrated at awaiting their turn for a place inside, some visitors got to work on the outside too; by the time the show closed, a dense pattern of multi-coloured graffiti – with the odd flower motif – had given the shed a distinctly urban look.

Taylor and Wood have a history of collaborating on wallpaper projects. Their first – in 1999 – was part of an installation at the Centre for Visual Arts in Cardiff. The paper, *When Ideas Become Pattern* – with its 'quaint' drawings of archetypal Welsh subjects (pit shafts, docks, chapels, farms, castles) printed in sepia tones – functioned as a subtle critique of the socio-economic shift from industry to 'heritage'. This process, by which vibrant productive cultures are emasculated, has resulted in the creation of a 'theme park' Britain where a sanitized and decorative version of the past is marketed to tourists and schoolchildren. The pair's most recent wallpaper design project is a specific response to some of the defining issues of our time. The global financial meltdown, the looming threat of environmental disaster, and the ever more intrusive apparatus of the state are addressed in three papers: *Blank Cheque, Crack* and *Witness*. These are currently being developed with assistance from Graham & Brown and may later be available commercially. *Witness* [Plate 76] is patterned with disembodied eyes, a reference to the ubiquity of surveillance; the walls not only 'have ears' (as World War II propaganda posters warned), they now have eyes too. The eyes themselves, reproduced from drawings, more than life-size, suggest an individuality and vulnerability that are negated by the unblinking scrutiny of the security camera and CCTV; conversely, they also remind us that the eye ('the window of the soul') is a marker of identity through iris pattern-recognition. The paper is being produced as a single-colour print, but also as a blown vinyl (a relief wallcovering made by printing with a vinyl ink containing a catalyst that expands when heated). Much used in the trade for textured papers, the blown vinyl process has not previously been exploited by artists.[58]

Artists have regularly taken conventional prosaic motifs and given them a new lease of life. Just as the cheerful floral pattern, a traditional staple of the wallpaper trade, has been worked over, so other motifs, not inherently decorative or associated with homeliness, have been infiltrating wallpaper design (and interior decoration more generally). The design studio Timorous Beasties have made something of a speciality of this, giving a twist to familiar patterns – as in *London Toile* [Plate 77] and the more recent *Devil Damask Flock* [Plate 78] – and also introducing unconventional motifs, such as bees, iguanas and B52 bombers. A new London company, De Angelis & Garner, has likewise devised wallpaper patterns from unlikely imagery – notably

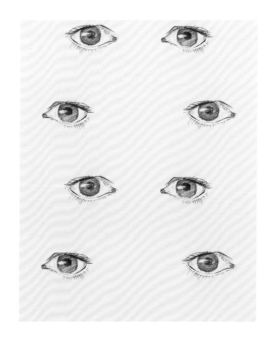

76. Chris Taylor & Craig Wood, *Witness*, 2009. Machine-printed wallpaper. Produced by Graham & Brown Ltd., Blackburn, UK. © Taylor & Wood, 2009

motifs derived from the distinctive features of influential punk/New Romantic performance artist Leigh Bowery (1961–94), as photographed by Kate Garner. In *Brilliant Me*, Bowery's head, with its exaggerated make-up, is repeated to appear as an exotic orchid-like flower, with a flavour of *fin-de-siècle* decadence.

In the same vein, Abigail Lane, working a part of a design collective Showroom Dummies, has made wallpapers commercially.[59] The group has so far specialized in producing wallpapers, fabrics, tiles and furniture printed with everything from dogs, bugs and lizards to erupting volcanoes [Plate 79] and frolicking skeletons; their first collection was called *Interior Motives (Natural Histories and Natural Disasters)*. The designs and the chosen motifs are dramatic, theatrical and provocative, though with an edge of humour. Lane likes the immersive quality of wallpaper, the way it surrounds the viewer so that 'like Alice in Wonderland, you're through the looking glass and into the story' in a very immediate way.[60] For Christmas 2004, Mulberry, a leather goods and accessories company, commissioned them to collaborate on specially designed interiors and window-dressing props for their retail outlets, as well as limited edition printed blankets available to buy. The Mulberry commission inspired Showroom Dummies to create folding Perspex screens, printed with life-size reindeer, and also a wallpaper, which looks at first sight like an elegant rococo-style abstract design, but up close, reveals itself as arrangements of bones – reindeer bones [Plate 80]. As in the work of the Dutch furniture makers Studio Job (pieces from their *Perished Collection* are inlaid with pictures of animal skeletons), the effect is not macabre but decorative and irreverent.

The designs of Showroom Dummies papers connect to the darker themes of fairy tales and gothic literature. This is a pronounced contemporary trend in art and design, embodied most vividly in much

of the work identified with the 'Design Art' phenomenon, where conventional furnishings are reimagined by their makers as extravagant and mostly impractical fantasies, retaining only vestiges of their original functions. The seductive *Fig Leaf* wardrobe (2008) of Tord Boontje (born 1968, Netherlands) reveals a narrative about the concept of clothing as prompted by Adam and Eve tasting the fruit of the Tree of Knowledge, but is of little practical use; his *Princess Chair*, flounced and frilled, has more to do with showing off than sitting down.[61] Likewise, when artists have turned to making wallpaper, the practical and decorative aspects of the medium are pertinent but often subordinate to this potential for narrative; sometimes these priorities may be explicit, sometimes allusive. Kiki Smith (American born 1954, Germany) recently produced a wallpaper (with Studio Prints, New Jersey) for an exhibition, *Her Home*;[62] it is now available commercially. A sculptor and innovative printmaker, Smith has often explored storytelling, connecting with nostalgia for childhood and reinventing myths and folk tales from a feminine perspective. In *Maiden & Moonflower* [Plate 81], a doll-like woman stands beneath a gnarled leafless tree populated with owls and moths, and surrounded by a scattering of stars. The naïve drawing and the disregard for perspective and scale are reminiscent of early woodcut illustrations, and the colourways – including 'Winterfrost', 'Moth', 'Dawn', 'Twilight' – evoke a world of magic.

—

It is impossible to discuss wallpaper – even in the contemporary context – without at some point mentioning the continuing influence of William Morris. Morris's papers – still in production, still in demand – are acknowledged as models of successful pattern design. Several of the artists who have made wallpapers have either acknowledged Morris, or engaged with his work directly: Thomas Demand's dense naturalistic ivy pattern referenced the foliage patterns characteristic of the Arts and Crafts

77. *London Toile*, designed and produced by Timorous Beasties, *c.*2005. © Designs by Timorous Beasties

78. *Devil Damask Flock*, designed and produced by Timorous Beasties © Designs by Timorous Beasties

79. Showroom Dummies,
Erupting Volcano, mural
wallpaper, 2003. Installation
view, skeleton tile fireplace,
Kings Cross, London, 2003.
Photo: Coco Amardeil

OPPOSITE:
80. Showroom Dummies,
Reindeer Bone wallpaper,
2004. Installation view,
Mulberry store, Bond Street,
London, 2004. Photo: Jan Von
Holleben

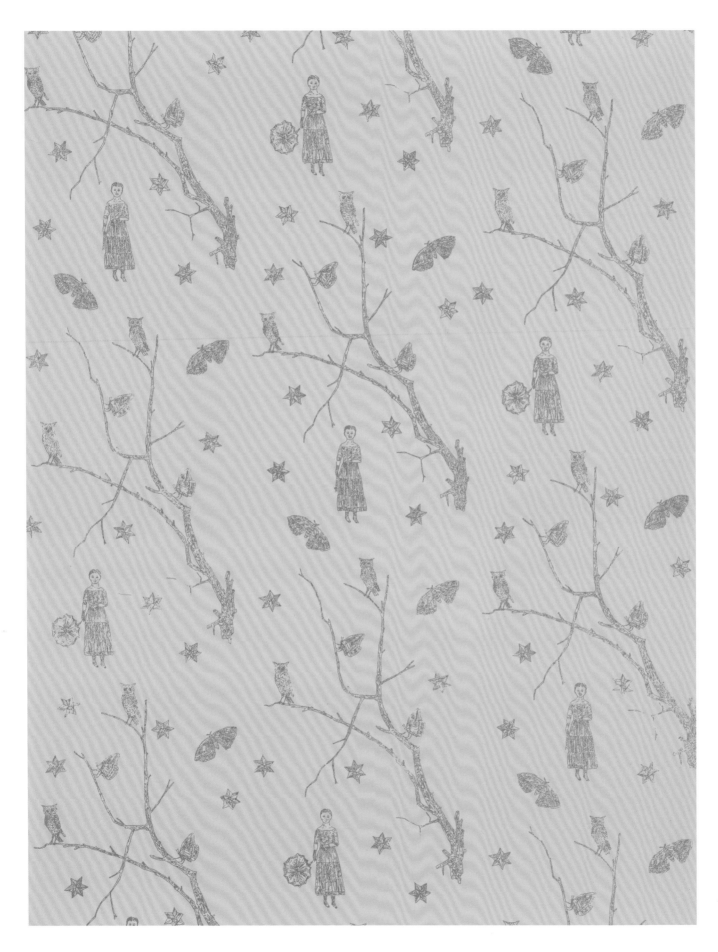

movement; Catherine Bertola remodelled Morris's *Marigold*, and others have appropriated Morris patterns to explore the nature of pattern. David Mabb (born 1959, UK), for example, has been for many years engaged in a kind of posthumous collaboration with Morris, using Morris fabrics and wallpapers as the grounds for formal experiments. Mabb's interest has focused not only on the structure of the patterns but also on the inherent contradictions between Morris's political beliefs – he was a campaigning socialist – and his practice as a designer and a businessman, who made a living creating handmade luxury goods for a wealthy clientele.

In a series of collage prints from 2006 Mabb contrasted the political philosophies and design practices of two artists – Morris and Alexander Rodchenko – who held socialist views and produced designs ostensibly intended to enhance the lives of the working classes. Each used pattern design to promote a different form of socialism and utopian enterprise. Morris's designs were hand-printed (and thus labour intensive and costly) and his flower and foliage patterns were suggestive of a nostalgia for rural life; Rodchenko, a member of the Russian Constructivist group, promoted a radical socialism and devised textile designs that were to be machine-printed (and thus cheap), with patterns based on commonplace utilitarian objects – such as beer bottles or 10-kopeck coins. Mabb copied Rodchenko's patterns and output them as digital prints (today's cheap and ubiquitous print medium); he then cut out the individual motifs and collaged them onto sheets of modern hand-blocked Morris wallpapers, crafting 'GM' hybrids that illustrate an awkward tension between the two designs and the philosophies that underpinned them [Plate 82].

Morris's designs have also been fertile sources for Christopher Pearson, who calls himself a 'digital craftsman'; he sees wallpaper as having the potential to teach, to entertain, and to migrate from walls to other surfaces and other structures. Pearson has made a number of

animations (including a wall-sized installation for Heathrow Terminal 5) in a series called *Look at Your Walls* (in reference to Morris's injunction on interior decoration, 'think first of the walls'[63]). *Willow Bough*, a Morris pattern from 1887, is the basis for an engaging animation in which the pattern is constantly reconfigured, as branches blow in the wind, flowers grow, birds and mice appear, and finally the leaves shrivel and die. Morris patterns were notable for their naturalism, so they lend themselves well to this playful narrative, which takes them back to nature. Other patterns have been brought to life including the sordid urban scenery of Timorous Beasties' *Glasgow Toile*. Already darkly ironic, in Pearson's version the implications of the original are acted out: a seagull is shot, a building collapses, and a blind man has an accident.

While not explicitly referencing Morris, the award-winning multimedia designer Daniel Brown (born 1977, UK) has designed what he calls Software as Furniture, animated digital imagery projected as wall-sized decorations that reflect his belief in 'a very traditional sense of beauty'.[64] The best known of these, his *Flowers* series [Plate 83], features generative synthetic floral imagery that 'grows' as we watch, subsuming the viewer in an enveloping environment, the visual analogy to ambient music. Brown's commissions for public spaces include *Waterfall* (2005) for the Park Hotel in Delhi; here a sequence of never-repeating kinetic waterfall patterns is generated on the wall. The patterns build up over several minutes before fading away.

Like Pearson, Erwan Venn has also brought wallpaper to life. He has made paintings inspired by wallpaper patterns, but has also explored pattern in more dynamic ways. *Destroy Wallpaper* (2006) [Plate 84] is a computer animation that shows a succession of patterns mutating or collapsing. There is a connection with natural processes of change and decay. At the same time the animations adapt the graphic language of computer games in which characters float or fly across the screen and are zapped by

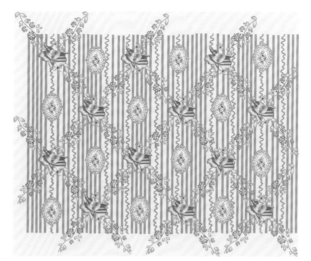

FAR LEFT:
83. Daniel Brown, Installation view, *Flowers* projection (from the series *On Growth and Form*), 2003. © The Artist. Northern Gallery for Contemporary Art

LEFT:
84. Erwan Venn, Still from *Destroy Wallpaper* animation, 2004. © Erwan Venn

the sharp reflexes of the player. Sometimes the destruction appears to be generated within, producing effects similar to that of a computer virus that causes text to 'fall' to the bottom of the screen.

Venn has also explored the analogies between wallpaper and music – the insistent rhythms of pattern and repeat – in *Shout & Yell: Memory & Patterns*, a series of diptychs that pair wallpapers with the lyrics of pop songs, feeding on a shared nostalgia to encapsulate the decades from the 1960s to the 2000s. The 'shining bright' and 'golden' faces of the Jam's 'In the City' find their echo in the yellow daisies of a grid-like floral paper in typical 1970s colours. The overblown materialistic optimism of our present decade is embodied in a retro psychedelic swirl set beside 'I Dreamed a Dream', an anthem from the musical *Les Misérables*, as sung by *Britain's Got Talent* phenomenon Susan Boyle.

—

Once found in almost every home, wallpaper has largely disappeared from the domestic setting as we have 'chuck[ed] out the chintz' (as suggested by the jingle to an IKEA TV ad campaign in 1996) in favour of a modified minimalism; wallpaper survives and thrives in National Trust houses and in hotels, shops, clubs and restaurants. It enjoys periodic revivals as fashions change: the bold orange and brown geometric patterns of the 1970s had a comeback moment recently, and stylists were hot-footing it to the vintage wallpaper shop E.W. Moore in East London to snap up rolls of period originals; the large-scale elegant retro designs of Cole & Son are also much in favour. Designers play on nostalgia with a twist, or on humour, irony and kitsch. Perhaps only artists (and curators!) are truly in love with wallpaper now. The phenomenon was celebrated with a major exhibition, *On the Wall,* at the Rhode Island School of Design and the Fabric Workshop Museum in Philadelphia in 2003. The Fabric Workshop has contributed much to the

rise of the artist's wallpaper, providing facilities, advice, and encouragement to several of the artists discussed here, including Green, Marti, Weems and Eisenman, and to many others.

Though we use less of it in our homes, wallpaper has become a ubiquitous feature of our visual economy – it is no longer simply a domestic decoration, indeed it is no longer merely wallpaper. Watch a TV interview with a football club manager or a Formula 1 racing champion, or the film of a politician on a podium – and the background is likely to be plastered with a repeating pattern: a 'wallpaper' of brand names and logos, aspirational but meaningless phrases, the corporate identity of a sponsor or the buzzwords of a campaign [Plate 85]. *Time* magazine noted this phenomenon in 2002, observing that the American government had 'made a habit of visual message bearing, regularly wallpapering the president's backdrop with the official theme of the day.'[65] Popular culture, political statement, fine art, advertising: wallpaper has come a long way since it left home and began making an exhibition of itself.

Gill Saunders

References

1   David Lomas has described Surrealism, with its self-consciously theatrical spaces, as a forerunner of installation art, and suggests that they share 'a conception of the artwork as a mise-en-scène of unconscious fantasies'. See *Subversive Spaces: Surrealism and Contemporary Art* (Manchester: Whitworth Art Gallery), 2009, p.21.

2   Harold Rosenberg, *The Tradition of the New* (New York: Horizon Press, 1959; London: Thames and Hudson, 1962), p.34.

3   John Updike, *Just Looking: Essays on Art* (New York: Knopf, and London: Deutsch, 1989), p.115.

4   Niklas Mak, in *Frankfurter Allgemeine Zeitung*, quoted in Luke Harding 'German Critic Attacks Turner Prize Winner', *The Guardian*, 7 December 2006, described Abts's paintings as looking 'like pattern samples from an old German Democratic Republic wallpaper factory'.

5   Judith Tannenbaum and Marion Boulton Stroud, *On the Wall: Contemporary Wallpaper* (exhibition catalogue, Providence: Rhode Island School of Design Museum of Art, and Philadelphia: Fabric Workshop and Museum, 2003).

85. Managing Director David Gill and Manager Sir Alex Ferguson with new goalkeeper Tim Howard at the press conference to announce his signing for Manchester United at Old Trafford on July 15, 2003 in Manchester, England. Photo by John Peters/Manchester United via Getty Images

6   Julie Mehta, 'Rolling out Wallpaper: Artists are Using Off-the-wall Techniques to Design Wallpapers that Demand Attention', *Art Business News*, February 2004.

7   The houses were demolished to make way for the M11 Link Road in East London. Smith, who lived in the locality, has made a number of films that have focused on the changing character of the area, and particularly its architecture and sense of community. See *John Smith: Film and Video Works 1972–2002* (Bristol: Picture This Moving Image and Watershed Media Centre, 2002).

8   Adolf Loos, *Ornament and Crime: Selected Essays*, edited by by Adolf Opel, translated by Michael Mitchell (Riverside, CA: Ariadne Press, 1998), pp.167–76 ['Ornament and Crime' first published 1908].

9   Le Corbusier, *Vers une architecture nouvelle*, Paris: Crès, 1923; translated as *Towards a New Architecture*, London: Rodker, and New York: Brewer and Warren, 1927; many subsequent editions.

10   Wyndham Lewis, interview with 'M.M.B', 'Rebel Art in Modern Life', *Daily News and Leader*, 7 April 1914.

11   Christopher Reed, 'Domestic Disturbances' in *Contemporary Art and the Home*, edited by Colin Painter (Oxford and New York: Berg, 2002), p.46.

12   In a manner analogous to 'design art', the work of designers whose shift from mass-produced artefact to unique crafted pieces, which has been the subject of much recent debate and promotion.

13   Thomas Hess, 'Andy Warhol', *Art News*, vol.63, no.9, January 1965, p.11.

14   Andy Warhol and Pat Hackett. *POPism: The Warhol '60s* (New York: Harcourt Brace Jovanovich, and London: Hutchinson, 1980), p.50.

15   Patrick S. Smith, *Warhol: Conversations about the Artist* (Ann Arbor, MI: UMI Research Press, 1988), p.217.

16   Nancy Spector, 'Robert Gober: Homeward-Bound', *Parkett 27*, 1991, p.83.

17   Sigmund Freud, *The Interpretation of Dreams*, translated and edited by James Strachey (London: Hogarth Press, 1953, New York: Basic, 1956) [first published 1899].

18   Richard Flood, 'Robert Gober: Special Editions, An Interview' (New York, 21 January 1990), *Print Collector's Newsletter*, March/April, 1990, pp.6–9.

19   'The habitat dioramas are among the greatest treasures of the American Museum of Natural History. Perhaps nothing embodies the spirit and mission of the Museum so completely as these amazing technical feats of illusion, which are recognized internationally as superb examples of the fusion of art and science.' Lewis W. Bernard, chairman of the American Museum of Natural History, on the Museum's website.

20   Richard Flood, op.cit., see note 22.

21   Robert Edis, 'Internal Decoration' in *Our Homes and How to Make Them Healthy* edited by S.F. Murphy (London: Cassell, 1883), p.356.

22   V&A, museum no.E.714–1952; see Gill Saunders, *Wallpaper in Interior Decoration* (London: V&A Publications, 2002), illus. p.134.

23   Richard Flood, op.cit., see note 22.

24   Indeed, for the artist Susan Hiller, who has used children's wallpapers as the 'ground' for painted works exploring automatism and the unconscious, wallpaper has the power to evoke 'the fearsome embrace of the nuclear family.' Lucy Lippard, 'Out of Bounds' in *Susan Hiller* (exhibition catalogue, London: Institute of Contemporary Arts, 1986), n.p.

25   'Hanging Man, Sleeping Man: A Conversation between Teresia Bush, Robert Gober and Ned Rifkin', *Parkett 27* (1991), pp.91–2.

26   See *Parkett 27*, op. cit., p.93.

27   Quoted in *Parkett 27*, op. cit., p.90.

28   Hearing of the Senate Judiciary Committee on the nomination of Clarence Thomas to the Supreme Court. Electronic Text Center, University of Virginia Library, 11 October 1991 (afternoon session).

29   Bruno Bettleheim, *The Uses of Enchantment: The Meaning and Importance of Fairy Tales* (London: Penguin, 1991), p.94 [first published 1976].

30   Illustrated in *The Image of the Black in Western Art*, vol.4: *From the American Revolution to World War I*, part 1, by Hugh Honour (Cambridge, MA: Harvard University Press, 1989).

31   *Projects: Carrie Mae Weems* (New York: Museum of Modern Art, 1995), n.p.

32   For an exhibition, *Patterns* (2001–02), at the Spacex Gallery, Exeter, Sedira papered one of the rooms with a geometric-patterned wallpaper; produced by Cole & Son, this design from *c.*1870–80 was inspired by the Islamic-influenced Elizabethan ceiling at Haddon Hall, Derbyshire, and demonstrated the way in which Islamic ideas have been integrated into Western culture over a long period.

33   Lachlan Blackley, *Wallpaper* (London: Laurence King, 2006), p.155.

34   V&A: E.474–1914. See Gill Saunders, op. cit., illus. p.86.

35   The Palestinian poet Mahmoud Darwish has written of 'the house as casualty' in the continuing conflicts in the Middle East: see *A River Dies of Thirst: Diaries* (London: Saqi, 2009).

36   Mrs Beeton, *Housewife's Treasury of Domestic Information* (London: Ward Lock, *c.*1865), p.211.

37   Quoted in Tom Lutz, *American Nervousness, 1903: An Anecdotal History* (Ithaca, NY: Cornell University Press, 1991), p.230.

38   Charlotte Perkins Gilman, *The Yellow Wallpaper and Selected Writings* (London: Virago, 2009) ['The Yellow Wallpaper' first published 1892].

39 Jeanne Nugent, curator of *Gender Engendered*, Community Education Center, Philadelphia, 1992, the exhibition in which Marti's wallpaper was first shown. Quoted by Richard Torchia in an unpublished press release.

40 *Beer Can Library* wallpaper first shown at Art Alliance, Philadelphia, October 1997.

41 Guy de Maupassant, *Bel-Ami*, translated by Douglas Parmée, London: Penguin, 1975, p.61 [first published 1885].

42 First shown at the Kunsthalle, Lucerne and subsequently at Karsten Schubert Gallery, London.

43 Leigh Hunt, *Autobiography* (3 vols, London: Smith Elder, 1850), quoted in E. A. Entwisle, *A Literary History of Wallpaper* (London: Batsford, 1960), p.71.

44 *Natural Dependency*, Jerwood Gallery, London, 3 November–12 December 1999.

45 The title, with its connotations of 'past, present and future' would seem to refer to the time-based nature of the installation.

46 'A Consuming Passion' (Anya Gallaccio in conversation with Francis Outred); see www.sothebys.com/café/Editorialsample.pdf

47 Sarah Lucas in conversation with James Putnam, January 2000, quoted at www.sadiecoles.com

48 Quoted in Damian Whitworth, 'Michael Craig-Martin: God of Small and Ordinary Things', *The Times*, 6 January 2009.

49 Quoted in Julie Mehta, op. cit.

50 *NewBuild: An Installation by Richard Woods* (with essay by Gill Saunders), Oxford: University of Oxford and New College, Oxford, 2005.

51 Woods quoted in *i-D* (The Aesthetic Issue), no.197, May 2000.

52 Thomas Hardy, *Far from the Madding Crowd* (London: Penguin 1978), chapter 35, p.295 [first published 1874].

53 Lisa Hecht in an unpublished artist's statement, May 2001, sent to the author.

54 Quoted in Sarah Bayliss, 'The New Art Wallpaper: It Doesn't Just Hang There', *The New York Times*, 29 June 2003.

55 V&A, museum no.E.1111–1921; see Gill Saunders, op.cit., illus. p.134.

56 Elphick quoted in *The Independent Weekend Review*, 10 April 1999, p.17.

57 Quoted at www.grahambrown.com/us/store/press_02.html

58 Information about Taylor and Wood's *When Ideas Become Pattern* and their project for *Walls Are Talking* is taken from email correspondence between the author and the artists, September 2009.

59 Showroom Dummies unites the complementary talents of Lane herself, fashion designer Brigitte Stepputtis, printer Bob Pain, and Edwin Wright, designer and maker of furniture and theatre props.

60 Quoted in Lachlan Blackley, op. cit., p.151.

61 See Gareth Williams, *Telling Tales: Fantasy and Fear in Contemporary Design* (London: V&A Publishing, 2009).

62 At Museum Haus Esters, Krefeld, Germany, 16 March–24 August 2008.

63 Quoted in A.V. Sugden and J.L. Edmondson, *A History of English Wallpaper 1509–1914* (London: Batsford, and New York: Scribner, 1926) as being part of Morris's lecture 'The Lesser Arts of Life', given in 1882.

64 Daniel Brown interviewed by Alex Haw for 'Kultureflash: Artworker of the Week #49', *Kultureflash*, no.128, 22 May 2005. See www.kultureflash.net/archive/128/priview.html

65 'Watch His Back', *Time*, vol.160, no.5, 29 July 2002, p.15.

Wallpaper, Wallpaper, Wallpaper:
Pattern, Repetition and Gender

When I was small I very much wanted a Barbie. I wasn't allowed one and instead was given a Sindy doll with short brunette hair – not quite so long-legged and platinum-locked (though hardly lacking in aspirational glamour in a fabulous green sequined disco playsuit) – perhaps a more accurate reflection of what I would grow up to look like. I remember gazing longingly at the rows of boxed, identical Barbies in the toyshop and on the bedroom shelves of other little girls; each equally tanned, blue-eyed and impossibly thin, always on tiptoe ready to don their high heels and dressed for an array of different fun feminine activities, such as sunbathing, shopping or going to a ball. Unabashedly tacky, Barbie seemed to be the essence of what was alluring about young America. *Barbie* wallpapers show her in a number of these different outfits, often surrounded by flowers or ribbons, repeated across the rolls. These rows of girls encapsulate that feeling I had in the toyshop: so many Barbies incessantly reaffirming that she is just what a girl should be. My parents were concerned about the influence Barbie would have on my self-image, but she was everywhere anyway, so substituting Sindy didn't shield me; it was just the idea of another possibility, a very small interruption of the pattern created by the sea of Barbies[1] [Plates 12, 86 and 87].

Any mass representation of bodies, like a best-selling doll or wallpaper decorated with girls, is a perfect crucible for reflecting and affirming – but also creating – values relating to appearance and behaviour. Can a novelty wallpaper contribute to this framing and reinforcing of gender roles? It seems so ephemeral and represents such a fleeting moment of childhood desire, yet its message is printed and consumed quickly and repeatedly. (Though often visualizing a short-lived interest, heavily patterned papers require a lot of work to strip off or cover over; they often linger on long after the appeal has worn off.) Beyond those aimed at children, since most wallcoverings are mass-produced and many are pictorial, we can find a wide spectrum of our society's visual preoccupations pictured in them. For example, our fascination with women's bodies and their adornment made representations of the female figure a popular choice for decorating walls in the latter half of the 20th century. There are wallpapers decorated with the male form, but these are far fewer. Attempting to represent them equally would give a false impression of the imbalance that exists in wallpaper history and in visual culture more broadly.

86. *Barbie*, late 1990s. Machine-printed wallpaper border. The Whitworth Art Gallery, The University of Manchester, W.1999.36

OPPOSITE:
87. *Sindy*, 1966. Machine-printed from surface rollers. The Whitworth Art Gallery, The University of Manchester, W.2000.107

Throughout its history wallpaper has largely been an imitative medium, designed to look like a textile or to give the impression of a garden or some other scene or surface. Where then does the trend for using female bodies as repetitive pattern on wallpaper originate from? Siegfried Kracauer, a German theorist, observed how, in mid-20th-century popular culture there was a shift from a focus on the individual performer to the use of multiple bodies in entertainment. He watched the dancing Tiller Girls and commented that they 'are no longer individual girls, but indissoluble girl clusters whose movements are demonstrations of mathematics'.[2] With their infinite patterns of people, the wallpapers discussed in this chapter clearly relate to Kracauer's lines of dancing legs, which he described as made up of 'sexless bodies in bathing suits'. But they were anything but sexless, they were the Tiller *Girls*, an ornamental sexualized spectacle characterized by the display and movement of their shapely feminine legs. Masses of gendered bodies have long been a common spectacle in entertainment and in everyday life: schoolchildren in uniform, soldiers marching, men in suits, girls on a night out and performers in identical costumes provide rich inspiration for the body multiplied as decoration.

All these people transposed into patterns connect with the idea that gender roles are created through repetition, particularly in the case of wallpaper, which is so much associated with repetitive designs. According to the influential theorist Judith Butler, gender identity can be seen as a pattern; it is not a natural and 'seamless identity', she argued, but more a 'compelling illusion'. Butler suggested that femininity or masculinity are performances we act out using a 'script' that has been repeated by previous performers through history, so 'the ground of gender identity is the stylized repetition of acts through time'.[3] Wallpaper is one small part of this visual 'script', repeating distinct messages to men and women.

So the candy-coloured *Barbie* wallpaper can be understood to repeat and reinforce patterns of gender representation, with all its archetypal ideas about female beauty as blonde, thin and white. Some artists have used the familiar and repetitive structure of wallpaper design to question these 'norms'. Equally candy-coloured and peppered with hearts and flowers (as well as with serpents), *Nana* was designed by the artist Niki de Saint Phalle in 1972. The 'heroine' recurring on this wallpaper – with black skin (in this colourway), generous thighs and uneven breasts – highlights the push towards women conforming to physical ideals and celebrates a different kind of beauty [Plate 88].[4] It has been noted by Sarah Wilson that Saint Phalle herself was a 'glamourpuss': a thin and gorgeous French archetype, attending fashionable private views and modelling for Vogue.[5] She made numerous Nanas, most of them sculptural, which have been interpreted as expressing anger about the cult of female beauty and the pressure on women to be ideal mothers: 'the Nanas are the monstrous, ugly, misshapen "other self", sticky with the "vicious" feminine… Is the Nana the "bad mother", a fearful effigy for Niki herself, who left her own two children and husband…?'[6] In these accounts Saint Phalle both gamely took part in and raged against what was expected of her as a woman. Her wallpaper pattern also contains a double-faced head, perhaps alluding to this conflict. *Barbie* wallpaper presents us with the building blocks of stereotypical gender roles in childhood; *Nana* confronts the complexity of adult experiences that struggle with these patterns learnt by children. The popular novelty and the art wallpaper are in conversation with each other, a pattern that will be seen again and again in the papers discussed here.

Toying with gender: Playboy in the bedroom

Where do these patterns begin? Children's and teen bedrooms are a key site for the construction of gender stereotypes; wallpapers designed specifically for children visualize the expectations imposed on little boys and girls. Another *Barbie* wallpaper depicts a series of ballerina Barbies in pink tutus striking a number of different poses [Plate 89]. Susan Leigh

BELOW:

90. *Manchester United Quad 4*,
1997. Machine-printed
wallpaper. Manufactured by
John Wilman Ltd. The
Whitworth Art Gallery, The
University of Manchester,
W.1997.47

Foster has written about the way in which the figure of the ballerina has become an aesthetic that conveys a gendered and racial ideal of physical refinement. She refers to the scores of girls donning pink tights and heading out to ballet classes everywhere from Hong Kong to New York: this is a global phenomenon, a pattern repeated the world over. On wallpaper ballerinas often appear as tiny, fairy-size girls (who can't be expected to eat much), contributing to the idea that small is feminine. There is currently an increasing social awareness of the ubiquity of eating disorders and body dysmorphia, particularly in women, and much debate about whether prolific media images of thin girlish beauty contribute to this. Additionally, through her tiny size, the ballerina conveys not just body aspiration but desire. Though he is not represented in most little girls' ballet-themed possessions, ballerinas are led around the stage by a male partner: '*She* is, in a word, the phallus, and he embodies the forces that pursue, guide, and manipulate it.'[7] This provides a further way of thinking about the repetitive patterns on children's wallpaper: do they also play their part in replicating the idea that heterosexual desire is perfect desire? Or, are these girls adopting poses for use in solos, which don't imply a male partner? If pursued beyond early childhood ballet becomes a tough physical activity in which girls often do better than boys, developing powerful bodies quite unlike the Tinkerbell ideal so often disseminated in media such as novelty wallpaper.

In 1997 John Wilman Ltd produced a *Manchester United Quad 4* wallpaper for boys at the same time as a *Spice Singles* paper, depicting the Spice Girls, aimed at girls [Plates 13 and 90]. The members of the team and the band are each reproduced with their signature next to them, creating a neat heterosexual mirroring between the designs. This is emphasized by the media-hyped relationship between David and Victoria Beckham, each appearing on their version of the wallpaper, the footballer and pop star performing the perfect part in a heterosexual contract.[8] Scores of other miniature figures, which children of both sexes watch on TV and play with, have been used to market wallpapers. *Batman* and *Gladiators* are two examples of television shows that have been merchandized as both dolls and wallpapers for boys [Plates 91 and 92]. Action words like 'Pow!' and 'Hang Tough' between the running, climbing, fighting figures emphasize the active masculinity of these heroes. Among the figures visual symbols such as clothes, weapons, flowers and colours each contributes to the insistent gendered messages.

91. *Batman*, 1966.
Machine-printed wallpaper.
Manufactured by Crown
Wallcoverings Ltd. The
Whitworth Art Gallery, The
University of Manchester,
W.1967.1093

92. *Gladiators*, 1992.
Machine-printed wallpaper.
The Whitworth Art Gallery,
The University of Manchester,
W.1995.7

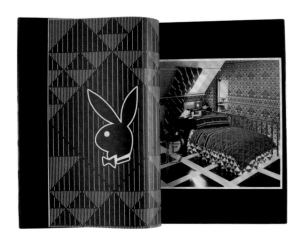

In numerous cases these symbols replace the use of the body to represent gender. A range of *Playboy* wallpapers aimed at teenage boys was produced by Crown Wallcoverings in the 1980s [Plate 93]. Photographs of room sets accompany each design in the pattern book. The famous *Playboy* bunny logo and masculine red, black and grey geometric shapes decorate the surfaces of each scheme. The sets contain incongruous combinations of possessions associated with boyhood and manhood. Champagne flutes, stilettos strewn on the floor and an exercise bike accompany the bunnies on wallpaper, curtains and duvet covers; the single beds, revealing the true target market, disrupt

this fantasy of a playboy's bachelor pad. This is a bedroom decorated as a space for private sexual fantasy and masturbation, perhaps with *Playboy* magazine or a similar publication to hand (the wallpapers are advertised by Crown as washable). The rabbit, the proverbial symbol of sexual freedom and activity, creates a repetitive sexual rhythm across this boys-own space. By association with a simple logo, recognizable because it is duplicated on a range of other merchandise, these wallpapers cash in on social aspirations to the lifestyle of the international playboy.[9]

The French artist Philippe Cazal creates work that plays with the meanings of visual signs in the media. Cazal's 2008 wallpaper *Le Lapin aux Oreilles Coupées* (which translates as 'the rabbit with the cut ears') uses the *Playboy* bunny logo to create a wallpaper pattern in a very similar style to the Crown range [Plate 94]. The large rabbit ears emblematic of *Playboy* are cut down (or castrated) to represent the loss of personal freedoms in contemporary society.[10] The artist uses wallpaper because it represents our exposure to multiple versions of the same message; he then disturbs the power of the familiar corporate symbol. Cazal's use of wallpaper highlights the nature of all of the children's wallpapers. Explicitly commercial, they look kitsch and dated very quickly; they reflect increasingly fleeting trends in popular culture. Yet though they are seemingly throwaway, and it is easy to deconstruct their blatant messages, they can be infinitely affecting in the formative years of their target market.

Women as wallpaper: Dominatrix in the bedroom

Gender roles or patterns have been seen to be an oppressive and restrictive structure by many feminist and queer theorists working on visual culture. From the 1970s there was a rejection by the women's movement of prevailing popular representations of female bodies. This questioned patriarchal structures in an attempt to break the cycle of

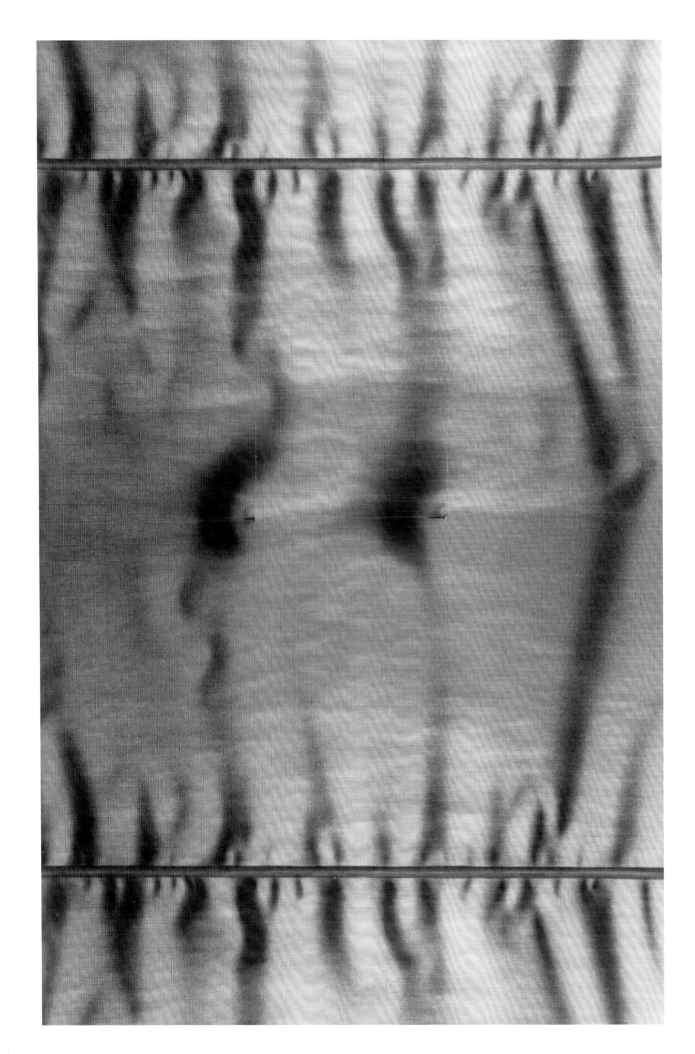

repetition of images that objectified women.[11] An extreme example of woman represented as a sexual or domestic object on wallpaper is *Right Hand Lady*, designed by the British artist Allen Jones for the German wallpaper company Marburger in 1972 [Plate 95]. Niki de Saint Phalle's *Nana* was part of the same Xartwalls range of papers, commissioned to update the image of this traditional manufacturer by selecting work by contemporary artists. Other papers in this range also depicted women, but none show men (though Peter Philips's *Kenya* is decorated with hyper-masculine motifs such as engines, roaring leopards and drill bits). *Faltenwurf* (a German word referring to the folds of hanging fabric) by Paul Wunderlich repeats a subtly erotic image in which a pair of disembodied breasts appear to be pushing through a drapery [Plate 96]. None is as visually direct as Jones's *Right Hand Lady*. Jones's wallpaper design was of a piece with his paintings, prints and sculptures, which took fetishistic depictions of women from popular media and reworked them in the context of fine art. Jones and Philips were part of the British Pop Art movement that, like its American counterpart, provoked a questioning of what was an appropriate subject for art.

Right Hand Lady depicts a dominatrix in leather or rubber underwear, long gloves and high-heel boots kneeling with a ring held out in her hand, as if for a subjugated sexual partner to jump through. Her breasts, bursting out above a tiny waist, reveal reddened nipples. She floats on a large painterly yellow brush stroke on a foil surface. Each figure fills the width of a roll and like a sex doll, the ultimate in woman reproduced as a sexual object, she is repeated along the length of the roll. This is not a pixie-size figure like those on the wallpapers for children; this girl is for adults and is almost large as life.

The depiction can be set in the context of a series of sculptures by Jones called 'Women as Furniture', which caused outrage in the women's movement in the 1970s. In an essay devoted to discrediting Jones's

work, Laura Mulvey wrote that: 'members of Women's Liberation noticed the exhibition and denounced it as supremely exploitative of women's already exploited image. Women used, women subjugated, women on display'. Mulvey used Freudian psychoanalytic theory to argue that it was driven by a castration complex, always avoiding the site of sexual difference, the lack of a phallus: female genitalia.[12] We move from papers dotted with phallic figures to one by an artist who is obsessed by their lack. No matter how provocatively posed and dressed, Jones's 'dolls' never have their genitals on display. In order to make this point and express the writer's outrage, Jones's work is reproduced again and again throughout Mulvey's article; she too uses visual repetition in order to denounce his message and emphasize her own.

Jones's use of wallpaper, like his use of furniture, can be understood as a referent to domestic spaces, an often-feminized sphere and frequently a site of female subordination. It is the fact that women are represented so directly as domestic objects that makes 'Women as Furniture' particularly shocking. Mulvey sums up the amalgamation of the domestic and the erotic: '…life-size effigies of women, slave-like and sexually provocative, double as hatstands, tables and chairs.'[13] Is his work an 'adult' version of the *Playboy* range by Crown, amplifying all the associations of the bachelor pad as a space for living out sexual fantasies? This effect is achieved not only by the sexualized figure but the 'confident' colours and the use of foil. Foil was a contemporary-looking surface effect, suggesting both luxury and modernity, and in choosing it Jones was probably making reference to other 1970s mass-market foil or metallic-looking wallpapers, also depicting sexualized women as pattern [Plate 97].

In recent years the fashion for reproducing retro-sexual images like these has increased. Publishers such as Taschen produce books and calendars of retro glamour girls like those on the foil wallpapers. Is this

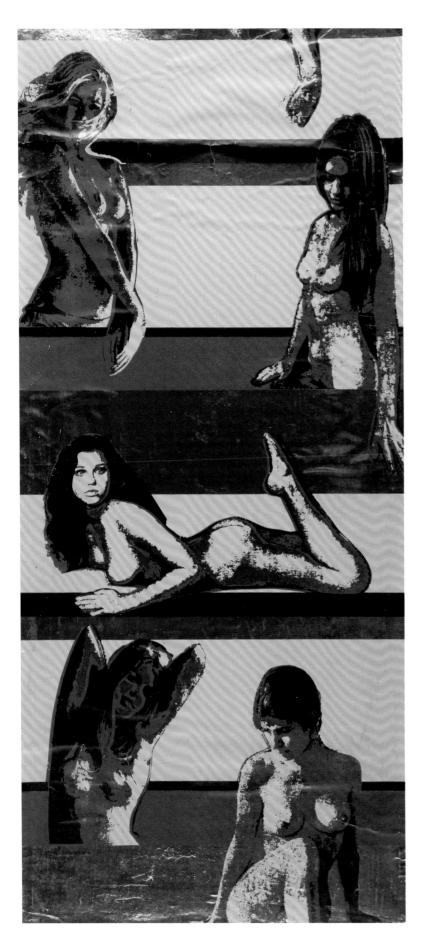

97. Wallpaper, 1970s. Hand screen-printed on paper-backed foil. The Whitworth Art Gallery, The University of Manchester, W.2008.124

just harmless nostalgia or a more alarming amnesia about the freedoms won by feminism? *Housewives* by Dupenny was designed in 2009 as a 'cheeky', kitsch revival of the 1950s housewife as pin-up [Plate 98]. The same company also produces *Burlesque* and *Call Girls* wallpapers, each one hand-drawn and hand screen-printed by the designer, Emily Dupen-Hopkins. Sexy girls engage in domestic chores such as baking, dusting and ironing. They turn to pout at the viewer in mildly provocative poses, revealing stockings and suspenders, a titillating rather than pornographic combination of the erotic and the domestic. Like Jones's dominatrix, each girl fills the width of a roll, making them hard to miss: they do not blend into the pattern. However, the emphasis here is on knowing humour rather than fetishistic objectification. The paper is also mainly aimed at a female consumer, perhaps with the intention of making mundane domestic chores seem a little more glamorous (Dupen-Hopkins has commented that it has been a very popular choice for kitchens and bathrooms).[14] The differences between *Housewives* and *Right Hand Lady* illustrate gendered tensions over the control (and design) of domestic space. Whichever wins, sleek bachelor pad or 1950s domestic perfection, pictures of girls make up the decorative scheme.

These visual domestic histories are not always referred to in such a nostalgic manner as *Housewives*. Like Allen Jones's dominatrix, the breasts in Sarah Lucas's *Tits in Space* wallpaper also float repeatedly on a blank surface and appear to be pneumatically inflated [Plate 58]. Matthew Collings has noted that the wallpaper has a 'sex/life/death theme: breasts made of cigarettes', but they are not cigarettes hanging alluringly from the plump lips of a sexy girl, they are squashed together and stained as if overflowing from an ashtray.[15] Lucas's work looks at sex, domestic and media life, but through a lens of banality. In stark contrast to the glamorized domestic/erotic depictions of Jones she looks more directly at these themes in their abject form; Lucas does not shy away

98. Emily Dupen-Hopkins, *Housewives*, 2009. Hand screen-printed wallpaper. Manufactured by Dupenny. © Dupenny. The Whitworth Art Gallery, The University of Manchester, W.2009.38

from representing a vagina as a kebab. Her work draws analogies between sex and filthy torn mattresses, stained toilets, stale food and worn out underwear.

Lucas's art has a lot in common with Robert Gober's, another artist who has used wallpaper to allude to domestic life. They both use furniture to address uncomfortable associations with private and sometimes oppressive experiences. In contrast to Jones's avoidance of the site of sexual difference, Gober's *Male and Female Genital Wallpaper* looks directly at it through a wallpaper covered with drawings of male and female genitalia [Plates 24 and 25]. When it was installed at the Paula Cooper Gallery in New York in 1989 several pewter plugholes were inserted in the wall and a bag of donuts sat on a pedestal in the middle of the room. This offered 'a paean to oral and anal appetites, an affirmation of sexual variousness… the antipode to the image of normative (hetero)sexuality'.[16] The homes these artists allude to are not freshly wallpapered and fetish-clean; the sex referred to is not an idealized fantasy. They use bodies on wallpaper to be provocative, but in a very different way from Jones.

Of course, not all domestic experience is horrifying. A work with parallels to Gober's *Male and Female Genital Wallpaper* embodies the idea that repetition can be comforting, secure and reassuring. Birth Rites is a collective that makes and collects artwork about childbirth. *Conception* arranges diagrams of male and female reproductive organs repetitively and perfectly fitted together in a gentle fleshy pink pattern [Plate 99]. This wallpaper is also about the association between the domestic, the erotic and reproduction, but presents it as something repetitively harmonious.[17] From the bluntness of *Right Hand Lady* to the serenity of *Conception*, all of these papers deal with the ongoing association of women and wallpaper with domestic space.

OPPOSITE:
99. Francesca Granato in collaboration with Helen Knowles, *Conception*, 2009. Hand screen-printed wallpaper. © Birth Rites Collection. The Whitworth Art Gallery, The University of Manchester, W.2009.39

BELOW:
100. Harry Cadney, *Superstar*, c.1974. Hand screen-printed on paper-backed foil. The Whitworth Art Gallery, The University of Manchester, W.1989.5

Art history in the bedroom

In his book *After the Great Divide*, about the difficult relationship between high art and mass culture, Andreas Huyssen has looked at the way that mass culture has been characterized as feminine and high culture as masculine (ideas that, he suggests, have lost their power only recently). Thus the fact that some wallpapers are art works and some are definitely not can be considered a gendered issue: a parallel binary that divides the pieces in question. Papers like *Gladiators, Spice Singles* or *Batman* were made purely for commercial purposes, while others, like *Le Lapin aux Oreilles Coupées* or *Tits in Space*, are wallpaper made for exhibition in a gallery context. (Several, like those in Marburger's Xartwalls range, also attempt to bridge the 'great divide'.[18]) Wallpaper has also regularly imitated art: *Superstar*, designed by Harry Cadney, explicitly echoes Andy Warhol's repetitive and iconic depiction of Marilyn Monroe [Plate 100]. This relationship has worked two ways: Warhol often took inspiration from the multiplication of goods and images for consumption; in turn, his depiction of Marilyn as pattern is mirrored back in popular print form in *Superstar*.

This says something about the position of a wallpaper collection within an art gallery. It is not a matter of 'lowbrow' items rubbing shoulders with the 'real' artworks; wallpapers have been demonstrated to have an imitated and imitative relationship with what constitutes art. In the end these objects are grouped here because, high and low, cheap or luxury, they are all wallpaper. Discussing or displaying them together lays bare the interdependence between art and commercial visual media. Does this also contribute to breaking down the 'great divide' as a gendered hierarchy? Or, does bringing Marilyn, almost the visual definition of the idea that blondes have more fun, into the hallowed gallery space simply strengthen the powerful gendered message from the merely popular to the highly serious? A wallpaper conceived by Warhol is obviously a more expensive and highly prized cultural commodity than a paper for

sale in a DIY store. Artists such as Gober and Lucas may tease out the meanings of gender stereotypes through the use of wallpaper, but Allen Jones and numerous others, with the clout of elite culture, have magnified and reinforced the power of those stereotypes.

Yet, in another form, 'she' (Barbie, Marilyn or Jones's dominatrix) was already there in the gallery before the interventions of recent decades. Art obviously exists as part of bigger histories of the visual; it has not been immune from the patterns and grooves of gender representation – quite the opposite in fact. In the scavenger-like quest for varied visual referents, wallpapers also use older art historical patterns of representation. For example, *Kate*, by the artist Edward Piper, was produced as part of a series of wallpapers conceived by Helen Feiler as art to paper the walls of ordinary homes [Plate 101]. Piper took his fascination with life drawing (particularly of women in coital positions) and splashed it repeatedly across his design. Each figure is partly obscured by inky stains that look like female genitalia.[19] (Here again repetition can be understood to allude to the repetitive motion of the sexual act.) The historic repetition of the female nude as a subject for art appears here as an unrelenting pattern over the space of a papered surface.

The male figure also has a long history in art, but one aligned less with sexual objectification. *Foule à Lier*, by the Belgian artist Charley Case, uses the repeated image of a nude male seen from behind, arms and legs spread to create a pattern that looks like a wire fence; this has suggestive associations of being caged in, or perhaps alludes to security and the comfort of structure [Plate 102]. Either way, the paper also makes oblique reference to an iconic image in art history, one that is reproduced and repeated endlessly on postcards, posters, in books, on the Internet, by people learning to draw and in innumerable other places: Leonardo da Vinci's *Vitruvian Man*. This illustration maps out the

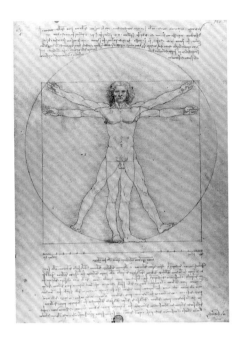

103. Leonardo da Vinci, *Vitruvian Man*, c.1487. Pen and ink with wash over metal-point on paper. Photograph: © Luc Viator GFDL/CC

ideal geometry of human proportions through diagrams of two superimposed figures [Plate 103]. Here we have a stereotype that creates a repetitive pattern across the world (telling us both what male bodily perfection and what artistic genius should be), in a fashion similar to the *Mona Lisa* – or to images of Marilyn Monroe.

Conclusion: towards 'a different sort of repeating'

This essay has been about bodies and faces, named or anonymous, so often reproduced that they create icons and clichés, particularly on wallpaper. These are easy to repeat, often easy on the eye, and are very hard patterns to break. It is not just on the surface of wallpapers that we find repetitive patterns of people. The way papers are made, stored and consumed also reflects the mass character of contemporary life. Returning to the rows of dancing girls, Kracauer observed: 'The regularity of their pattern is cheered by the masses, themselves arranged by the stands in tier upon ordered tier'.[20] Kracauer suggested that differences between human beings were increasingly standardized for use within the machine of the capitalist system. As well as the ordered rows of people in the audience he compared the legs of the dancing girls with the production line of hands and bodies working in a factory.[21] Wallpapers were traditionally made in factories 'manned' by rows of bodies, but today newer technologies are automating and depopulating the production process. Still though, sheet upon sheet, roll after roll, they are printed in our 'age of mechanical reproduction'.[22] When in storage behind the scenes in a museum (or in a shop storeroom), roll after roll, box after box, drawer after drawer line up to create another even pattern of wallpaper in specially designed supports and racks [Plate 104].

When choosing wallpapers for viewing or display from these seemingly endless ordered rows of choices, careful consideration needs to go into how to represent their meanings. Do we want to disrupt the patterns

they repeat, and if so, how? The artists who use wallpaper have also tackled this question. But, of course, wallpaper is not usually made with this purpose in mind. Paradoxically, by making it art, wallpaper is removed from the very domestic context the artists so often evoke with it. Wallcoverings are far more regularly chosen for decorating rooms than for display in art galleries. Furthermore, it is not only those with a public profile who have the potential to question the patterns wallpapers repeat: not every little girl wants a Barbie wallpaper. 'Un-public' choices about how to decorate domestic spaces are made everyday. The small boy, the old lady, the businessman, the housewife all have historic layers of gendered examples laid out before them. Judith Butler argues that we have some choice in the way we perform the 'script' presented to us. It may be acted out in various ways: there is 'the possibility of a different sort of repeating, in the breaking or subversive repetition of that style'.[23] So, then, if an elderly lady chooses to buy *Right Hand Lady* for her bedroom wall, does its meaning become quite different?

Dominique Heyse-Moore

References

1   Mary F. Rogers has argued that though Barbie can be considered an icon of racism, sexism and consumerism, her sexual identity and class are ambiguous, so her meanings are not wholly clear-cut. The issues of social class, what kind of homes the papers were used in and how they ended up in an art gallery collection, are significant ones, but are beyond the scope of this essay. Mary F. Rogers, *Barbie Culture* (London: Sage, 1999).

2   Siegfried Kracauer, *The Mass Ornament: Weimar Essays* edited by Thomas Y. Levin (Cambridge, MA: Harvard University Press, 1995), p.75.

3   Judith Butler, 'Performative Acts and Gender Constitution: An Essay in Phenomenology and Feminist Theory', *Theatre Journal*, vol.40, no.4, December 1988, p.520.

4   *Nana* was available in several colourways.

5   Sarah G. Wilson, 'Tu es moi: The Sacred, the Profane and the Secret in the Work of Niki de Saint Phalle' in *Niki de Sainte Phalle* edited by Simon Groom (London: Tate Publishing, 2008), p.17.

6   Ibid. Niki de Saint Phalle left her family to live and work with the artist Jean Tinguely, whose work was also used as a wallpaper in the Xartwalls series.

7   Susan Leigh Foster, 'The Ballerina's Phallic Pointe' in *The Feminism and Visual Culture Reader* edited by Amelia Jones (London and New York: Routledge, 2003), p.434.

8   The Spice Girls were marketed with the tagline 'Girl Power', an example of feminist ideas, albeit in a skewed form, creeping into popular culture. Another Spice Girls wallpaper depicts them cavorting on a bed, a girls' bedroom idealized as a celebrity slumber party.

9   The 1966 James Bond wallpaper works in a very similar fashion, glamourizing 007 with the visual shorthand of girls, guns and cars [Plate 14].

10   PDF about the exhibition of *Le Lapin aux Oreilles Coupées* at Galerie Georges Verney-Carron in Lyon in 2008 http://www.philippecazal.com/details_categorie.php?index=1&id=162

11   See Amelia Jones's outline of the debates and work that was produced during this period: 'Body' in *The Feminism and Visual Culture Reader* edited by Amelia Jones (London and New York: Routledge, 2003), pp.369–71.

12   Laura Mulvey, 'You Don't Know What is Happening, Do You, Mr Jones?', *Spare Rib*, no.8, 1973, pp.127–31.

13   Mulvey also notes that the original *Chair* is now owned by a German business tycoon 'whose complacent form was recently photographed for a *Sunday Times* article, sitting comfortably on the upturned and upholstered female figure.' Ibid., p.13.

14   http://www.dupenny.com

15   Matthew Collings, *Sarah Lucas* (London: Tate Publishing, 2002), p.17.

16   Lynne Cooke, 'Disputed Terrain' in *Robert Gober* edited by Judith Nesbitt (exhibition catalogue, London: Serpentine Gallery, and Liverpool: Tate Gallery, 1993), p.22.

17   Another piece by Birth Rites, *Childbirth*, refers to the exploitation of women through visual reference to prostitutes' calling cards, combined with birthing positions, arranged to look like a traditional wallpaper pattern if viewed from a distance. http://birthrites.org.uk/

18   Andreas Huyssen, *After the Great Divide: Modernism, Mass Culture, Postmodernism* (Bloomington: Indiana University Press, 1986; London: Macmillan, 1988).

19   The artist Abigail Lane created a wallpaper using imprints of a female bottom in *Bottom*, 1992 [Plate 49].

20   Siegfried Kracauer, op. cit, p.76.

21   Ibid., p.78.

22   Walter Benjamin, 'The Work of Art in the Age of Mechanical Reproduction' in *Illuminations*, edited by Hannah Arendt (London: Pimlico, 1999), pp.211–44.

23   Judith Butler, op. cit. Butler has also suggested that gender is performed under duress because of the negative consequences for those who break the established pattern. She gives the example of a transvestite who is applauded as a performer on stage but experiences rage, fear and even violence while travelling home on a bus.

104. Mobile storage racks in the Wallpaper Study Room, 2004. The Whitworth Art Gallery, The University of Manchester

Wallpaper, Dust and 'Muck of that Sort': Themes in the Work of Catherine Bertola

Now here's my trouble. I don't believe the human race is capable of such a sacrifice. I believe it will still demand wallpapers and muck of that sort, and patterns on biscuit boxes.[1]

Writing on the comparable merits of hand and machine production in 1948, Eric Gill, the pre-eminent British typographic designer of his generation, drew together some complex and deeply-seated assumptions and values. Gill was a designer/craftsman, schooled in the ethos of the Arts and Crafts traditions, and subsequent Modernist philosophies, and it is certainly not surprising to find him expressing his ideas on the subject in terms of a 'troubled' lack of faith in the human capacity for judgement, or perhaps even 'sacrifice'. Gill was certainly not alone in placing the blame for what he clearly perceived as 'inferior' things at the door of the consumer. Indeed, in doing this he perpetuated a longstanding tradition of professional, masculine, design discourse that located all of its ills within the realm of consumption.

To find the example of wallpaper firmly embedded within this rhetoric is of little surprise either. Wallpaper, an object so deeply implicated within debates about different modes of manufacture and their relative 'qualities', about taste and judgement, fashion and style, is perhaps the bogeyman of all Modernist, rationalizing sensibilities. Without any ostensible function beyond simply 'decoration', wallpaper constitutes the guilty vice of the homemaker. It is a material through which homes are made, and are made visible, and perhaps most importantly, a material through which they are changed. In this sense, wallpaper becomes not just some measure of household taste, but a salient record of time's passing that speaks not just of the history of a room or a building, but of the moments and lives of the people who lived there. This is, I think, the artistic terrain of Catherine Bertola.

Along with objects and materials such as lace, textiles, paint and dust, wallpaper has offered Bertola a substance through which to investigate the ways things and spaces are made, and, in turn, the ways these things and spaces 'make' the lives lived through and with them. This concern with the often mundane materials and objects of everyday life belies a preoccupation with the ways in which time and the passing of time become inscribed and materialized in the things around us. Not surprisingly, much of Bertola's work has focused on the aesthetic conditions and experiences of the domestic interior, and the 'home' has provided her with a rich theme through which to explore issues of inhabitation, memory and place.

As the art historian Christopher Reed has long argued, art and domesticity have a problematic coexistence and too often the relationship is one of exclusion.[2] For Reed these are entirely modern circumstances:

> Domesticity, in short, is a specifically modern phenomenon, a product of the confluence of capitalist economics, breakthroughs in technology, and Enlightenment notions of individuality.[3]

According to Reed, the 'modern' and 'avant-garde' mode of fine art practice is centred on the values of 'masculinity, dynamism, individualism', and he has suggested that the home is neither the subject nor the location for this practice. Even in instances where Pop and later Postmodern artists such as Andy Warhol, Richard Hamilton, Bruce Nauman and Rachel Whiteread have brought art and domesticity together in their work, Reed has argued that the Modernist over-determined 'proscription' of fine art practice still continues to lead artists away from the pejorative associations of 'femininity, stasis, conformity, and the collectivity of family' so fundamentally linked to the home.[4]

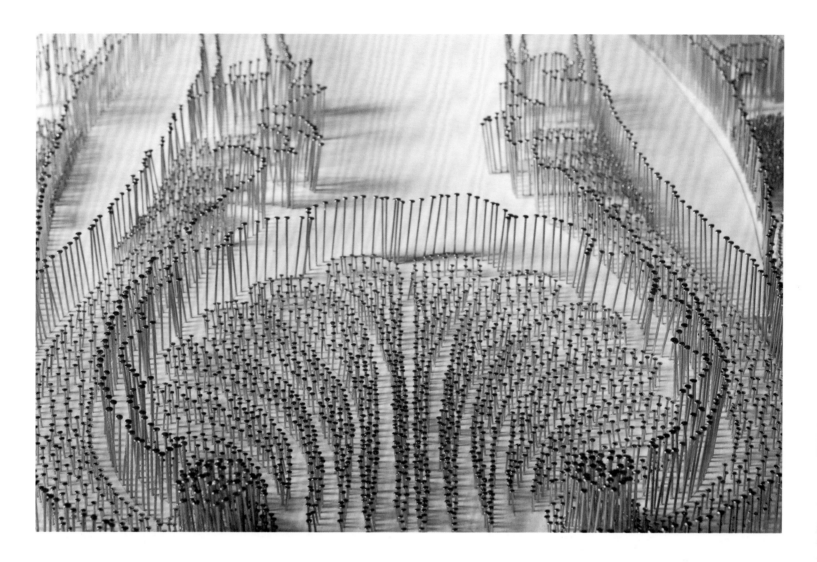

At the heart of this avant-garde proscription in recent years has been a determined emphasis on notions of 'concept', arguably at the expense of both the visual and material constitution of art. Indeed, popular notions of 'art' are too often and too easily dismissed as 'merely' conceptual. In contrast, Bertola's art is concerned quite fundamentally with the processes of making and materiality. This point is made not to suggest in any way that her work is without concept, rather that the critical and conceptual frameworks of her work are achieved through a deep and inquisitive engagement with the nature and processes of making. Whether concerned with the making of objects, such as stainless steel cutlery or ladies lace knickers, or of the spaces, boundaries and thresholds of the home, her body of work to date is characterized by an in-depth process of research as creative practice.

For her recent contribution to the *Out of the Ordinary* exhibition at Sheffield's Millennium Gallery, Bertola was invited to create a work in dialogue with the Sheffield Museum's existing collection of objects.[5] Not surprisingly, her work centred on the 'hidden' processes 'behind' the objects of the collection and she focused her attentions on the traditions and working practices of the dwindling Sheffield plate industry. Looking beyond the finished surfaces of the museum objects, Bertola sought out

the tools and other working objects that had been used to create them. Ultimately, *Bit by Bit, Piece by Piece* (2009) [Plate 105], was made over a lengthy period of time, using stainless steel dressmaking pins, perhaps the very foundational increment of Adam Smith's 18th-century vision of an industrial world. This work delicately replicates a pattern based on traditional cutlery handle designs, to create a large-scale carpet. The carpet, the product of a quite painstaking and repetitive process of manual and dexterous labour, embodies Bertola's fascination with the intricate and detailed stages of making.

In a subsequent commission, for *Beyond Pattern* at the Oriel Davies Gallery in Newtown, Wales, elements of Bertola's work were in fact made by the collective labour of local residents in an approximation of the divided labour characteristic of industrial manufacture. The work, *From the Palace at Hillstreet* (2009) [Plates 106 and 107], featured a 'reproduction' of a carpet designed by Robert Adam, and required Bertola to redraw the design into over 90 separate sections of approximately 6 x 7 inches in size. Each of these sections was sent to participating volunteers, with clear instructions, a sewing frame and the correct tapestry wools. This process of 'dispersed' labour required a degree of 'design' and 'control' in the making not unlike the industrial

process of divided labour, in which creative invention and design are determined entirely at the outset of the work and the stages of its realization are mapped out in a sequential, ordered and potentially 'alienating' pattern.

The original carpet was designed by Adam for the home of Elizabeth Montagu, the venue of the Bluestocking Society gatherings founded in the 1750s. The privileged members of this elite gathering were dedicated to the education of women and are represented in the work by 12 drawings of Bertola's own legs wearing a different pair of intricately drawn contemporary lace tights. In this work we find pattern being used to signify both the invisible labours of the working female body in the form of the reconstructed carpet, and the intellectual capacities and ambitions beyond the traditional sphere of feminine accomplishments as manifested by the 'stocking' legs: the work moves seamlessly from the surface of the room to the surface of the body. This juxtaposition of the labouring and non-labouring productive female body echoes throughout Bertola's work. Not just because she herself is a physically labouring, working woman but because so much of what she concerns herself with, primarily the domestic space, is historically and culturally encoded as female.

As the other contributions to this book have made clear, the domestic interior, its decoration, furnishings and objects, has provided something of a focus for many contemporary fine artists over the past ten years. Artists have frequently chosen to transgress any notional separation of public and private spheres in order to create work that provocatively juxtaposes domestic concerns with those of a world 'out there'. In this sense many fine artists have sought to bring 'home' the public concerns of AIDS, war, terrorism or urban decay by puncturing the supposed sanctity of the domestic space. As *Walls Are Talking* makes abundantly clear, wallpaper has figured significantly in this work.

It could be argued, however, that for many artists wallpaper constitutes little more than a culturally 'placed' blank canvas. In its ubiquitous banality, so effectively described by Gill Saunders in this volume, artists have found a vehicle through which to establish and critique themes and ideas entirely external to the nature and conditions of wallpaper itself.

While the challenge posed by these works is the very bread and butter of contemporary fine art practice, it could be argued that such work simply perpetuates, quite 'loudly', a further marginalization of the home and domestic culture as discussed already above. The ubiquity of wallpaper is celebrated by these artists because of its ability to carry an unsuspected, challenging and disturbing message into the domestic space. In this sense, wallpaper really does act as a means of communication – where meaning is created at least in part through a dynamic juxtaposition of 'content' and 'form'. These 'big' themes come into view only on closer inspection of the wallpaper surface – something, in fact, rarely done. After all, who would think to look for 'meaning' in wallpaper? This conceit is perhaps at the centre of the visual encounter with artists' wallpaper.

With only a few notable exceptions this artistic engagement with wallpaper has been an almost entirely visual one, the material consideration of wallpaper as an object in its own right being fairly limited. This is perhaps not surprising, given that wallpaper is and has always been understood as essentially surface, something that covers something else. However, the materiality, weight and texture of wallpaper is fundamental to any cultural understanding of it. Indeed, it is the materiality of wallpaper in combination with its visual character that usually places it as commoditized 'product' of some process of manufacture. In the common parlance of the wallpaper marketplace, often weight = worth.

108. Catherine Bertola,
If Walls Could Talk…, 2002.
Found wallpaper in empty,
now demolished tower block,
Liverpool. Courtesy the artist
and Workplace Gallery

BELOW:
109. Catherine Bertola,
Switched, 1999. Graphite
powder, fablon, paper
mounted on MDF. 13 x 14cm.
Photo: Colin Davison.
Courtesy the artist and
Workplace Gallery

The materiality of wallpaper has long been key to Bertola's use of it in her work, and this is perhaps most apparent in her 2002 project *If Walls Could Talk…* [Plate 108], which saw her take up residency in a condemned tower block in Liverpool. Using a scalpel she painstakingly traced out the leaf pattern of the plain white-painted textured wallpaper that covered a room in one of the derelict flats. The effect of this was to peel the leaves away from the flat surface of the wall into an enhanced three-dimensionality. The effect of this work was striking, as if the paper leaves, left unattended by the now absent inhabitants of the room, had, like real leaves, taken on a life of their own and begun the process of reclaiming

the space from the man-made world. In this work, Bertola's restrained and fairly minimal intervention offered an animated disruption to the space that was is some sense in keeping with the wallpaper's original aspiration for texture and relief. This magical and quite beautiful quality was enhanced because the intervention itself was entirely fleeting and temporary in nature, the building eventually having to be demolished.

In her essay 'Dream Houses: Installations and the Home' Gill Perry has argued that the use of fine art installation practices demands 'a critical awareness of ideological contexts and relationships between viewers and objects',[6] and it is perhaps this critical awareness that makes installation such a potent strategy for artists working with the home. Citing Walter Benjamin's famous declaration that 'to live is to leave traces', Perry provides a very neat description of what might compel artists to work with the home:

> A home does not simply specify where you live; it can also signify who you are (socially, economically, sexually, ethnically) and where you 'belong' (geographically, culturally). And a house or a dwelling is full of the occupant's corporeality, of sleeping, eating, loving: of its existence as a home. Moreover, a house contains evidence of the intimate relationship between space and time. While the space of the constructed building may shelter people or families over long periods of time, the evidence of more transitory individual lives is visible in traces in and on the building and its furniture. These 'traces' may take the form of damage, dirt, dust, decorations, scratches, repairs and so on.[7]

The physical intervention in domestic space and on the surfaces of that space becomes a temporal one provoking the viewer to consider the nature of change and inhabitation. These themes are particularly notable in one of Bertola's early works, *Switched* (1999) [Plate 109],

which presented 13 prints 'captured' using graphite powder from the light switches in her own home. Focusing on that functional part of the domestic wall, the part often entirely undecorated by wallpaper or paint and that is touched repeatedly without thought or consideration many times a day, forces the viewer to consider their own light switches, perhaps for the very first time. This act of 'tracing' time was used by Bertola on a much larger scale more recently in her piece *Been and Gone* (2008) [Plate 110], which saw her return to the themes of spatial presence and absence by inscribing the plans and drawings of an old bus station on the walls of the Artium Museum in Vitoria-Gasteiz, Spain, which is built on the site where the station once stood. This work demonstrated an atavistic concern for memory, place and, perhaps most importantly, the often quick process of forgetting that happens when a new building literally erases the memory of an old one.

'Time', then, whether as a document of human labour or the 'useful' lifespan of an object or building, is a quite fundamental concern of

Bertola's art. Often work such as *Everything and Nothing* (2007) [Plate 111], presented at the Victoria and Albert Museum, emerges over the duration of an exhibition or residency as a unfolding record of labour, and few of the works survive in their original form beyond the period of their exhibition. To be 'fleeting' and 'ephemeral' is perhaps to capture something of Bertola's concern with the nature of change, transition and memory. In works such as *Hearth* (1999) [Plate 112], *Sweeping It Under* (1999) [Plate 113] and *After the Fact* (2006) [Plate 114] Bertola uses household dust, the very material of time's passing, to create suggestive interventions that evoke the surfaces and qualities of earlier, more pristine spaces. Invariably these interventions take the form of pattern, of carpets, lace curtains, and of course wallpapers, and this recurrent use of pattern, to 'set scenes' continues the deeply narrative quality of Bertola's work.

In its emphasis on the processes of memory, narrative and evocation Bertola's work can be viewed alongside that of Louise Bourgeois, Doris Salcedo, and Rachel Whiteread. Each of these artists has made work that

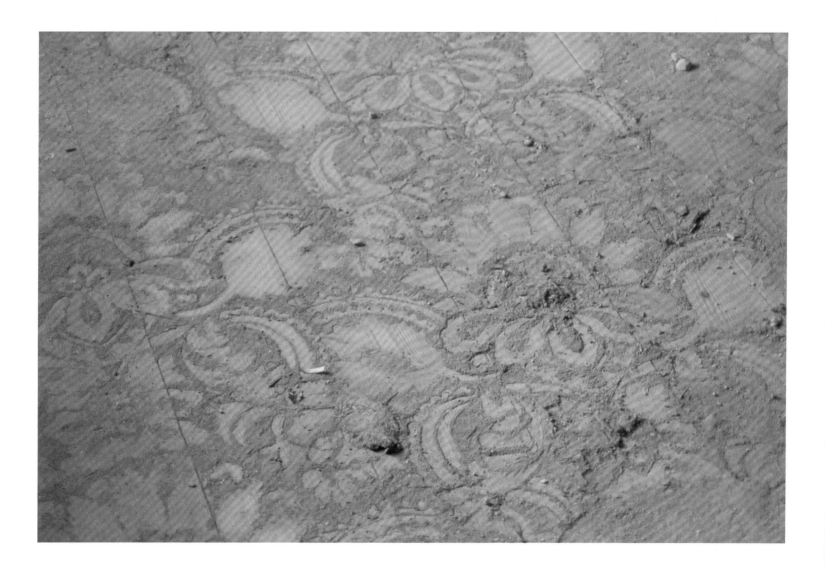

deals explicitly with the conditions of domesticity, narrative and biography, but much of this work has arguably been concerned in some way with rendering the home 'uncanny', causing it to become potentially alien, displaced and disoriented.[8] This is a strategy in marked contrast to that employed by Bertola, whose art never works 'against' its subject. Bertola's art works within the rhetoric and materiality of domesticity, not in order to undermine it, but to search out its subtleties and deepen the viewer's relation to it. It does this through a materialized narrative.

Gareth Williams has drawn on the work of Walter Benjamin to explore the role of narrative in relation to art/design objects. In *Telling Tales: Fantasy and Fear in Contemporary Design*, Williams has noted Benjamin's argument that storytelling and making objects are aspects of the same process:

> In fact, one can go on and ask oneself whether the relationship of the storyteller to his material, human life, is not in itself a craftsman's relationship, whether it is not his very task to fashion the raw material of experience, his own and that of others, in a solid, useful and unique way.[9]

This equation of the storyteller and craftsman seems particularly apposite to characterizing Bertola's work, as this work is defined by the unfolding process of its creation. In fact, it could be argued that her work almost resists some final moment of completion, that it remains always 'open'.

In her contribution to the exhibition catalogue *Psycho Buildings*, Jane Rendell reconsiders the notions of the 'open work' proposed by Umberto Eco in the early 1960s. Suggesting that Eco's concept of an 'open' artwork – one that requires imaginative completion by the viewer – anticipated discussion of relational aesthetics by three decades, Rendell argues that 'in demanding imaginative as well as perceptual and conceptual modes of use, these works are inhabited both consciously and unconsciously.'[10] In this manner, Bertola's use of domestic materials, patterns and aesthetics offers both an imaginative and reflective 'opening' to the viewer. The work demands an often poetic completion, and achieves this by an almost reminiscent suggestion of places and things once known. The works seem to be poised at the cusp between fact and fiction, imagination and memory, consciousness and unconsciousness.

LEFT AND OPPOSITE:
115. Catherine Bertola,
Beyond the Looking Glass
(Study 1), 2009. Paper.
Courtesy the artist and
Workplace Gallery

And so to *Beyond the Looking Glass*, in which Bertola turns explicitly toward the worlds of fiction and imagination [Plate 115]. Taking its cue from the fictional wallpapers documented only in the pages of classic novels, the work 'visualizes' for the very first time wallpapers previously unseen. Using the Wallpaper collections of the Whitworth Museum as a source of reference against which to 'interpret' the written design, Bertola provides a mediation somewhere between fact and fiction, which, like its written 'original', avoids all material form, having been drawn directly on the wall.

At the heart of all of Bertola's work is a deep concern for the ways in which pattern and surface mark out the nature of place, and this gives her art a very definite and particular aesthetic. To bring pattern and order to 'dust', the very disturbing matter responsible for disorder, decay and disarray, is in many ways a highly provocative thing to do, in that it forces people to see beyond commonly held perceptions of dust as 'dirt'. To then use this material to recreate the delicate patterns and surfaces of wallpapers and carpets, domestic objects often held up by the likes of Eric Gill and so many others before and after him as responsible for the aesthetic disorder, decay and disarray of our homes, and in turn our society, is to draw together a complex of deeply-seated social and cultural attitudes that accord certain objects, materials and places very certain and particular values. And to do all this within the rarefied spaces of the art gallery and the museum is to collapse any sense of the public and private realms with such quiet vitality that it feels at once both challenging and comforting. Whether she is working with dust or wallpaper or 'muck of that sort', Catherine Bertola is an artist whose work often gets her hands dirty.

Trevor Keeble

References

1   Eric Gill, *Letters of Eric Gill*, edited by Walter Shewring (London: Cape, 1947, New York: Devin Adair, 1948), quoted in E. A. Entwisle, *A Literary History of Wallpaper* (London: Batsford, 1960), p.179.

2   Christopher Reed (editor), *Not at Home: The Suppression of Domesticity in Modern Art and Architecture* (London: Thames and Hudson, 1996).

3   Christopher Reed, 'Domestic Disturbances' in *Contemporary Art and the Home*, edited by Colin Painter (Oxford and New York: Berg, 2002), p.35.

4   Ibid, p.46.

5   *Out of the Ordinary* was originally shown at the V&A, 13 November 2007–17 February 2008. See *Out of the Ordinary: Spectacular Craft*, edited by Laurie Britton Newell (London: V&A Publications, 2007).

6   Gill Perry, 'Dream Houses: Installations and the Home' in *Themes in Contemporary Art*, edited by Gill Perry and Paul Wood (New Haven and London: Yale University Press in association with the Open University, 2004), p.234.

7   Ibid, p.237.

8   Sigmund Freud, 'The "Uncanny"' in *Art and Literature*, edited by Albert Dickson (The Penguin Freud Library, vol.14; London: Penguin, 1985).

9   Walter Benjamin, quoted in Gareth Williams, *Telling Tales: Fantasy and Fear in Contemporary Design* (London: V&A Publishing, 2009), p.12.

10 Jane Rendell, 'Art's Use of Architecture: Place, Site and Setting' in *Psycho Buildings: Artists Take on Architecture*, edited by Ralph Rugoff (exhibition catalogue, London: Hayward Publishing, 2008), p.43.

Bibliography

Attfield, Judy, 'FORM/female FOLLOWS FUNCTION/male: Feminist Critiques of Design' in *Design History and the History of Design*, by John A. Walker and Judy Attfield, London: Pluto, 1989

Attfield, Judy and Pat Kirkham (editors), *A View from the Interior: Women and Design*, revised edition, London: Women's Press, 1995

Une Aventure de papier peint: la Collection Mauny (exhibition catalogue), Nantes: Conseil général de Loire-Atlantique, 1997

Bachelard, Gaston, *The Poetics of Space*, translated by Maria Jolas, New York: Orion Press, 1964

Banham, Joanna (editor), *A Decorative Art: 19th Century Wallpapers in the Whitworth Art Gallery* (exhibition catalogue), Manchester: Whitworth Art Gallery, 1985

Baudrillard, Jean, *Simulacra and Simulation*, translated by Sheila Faria Glaser, Ann Arbor: University of Michigan Press, 1994

Benjamin, Walter, 'The Work of Art in the Age of Mechanical Reproduction' in *Illuminations*, edited by Hannah Arendt, London: Pimlico, 1999, pp.211–44 [written 1935; first published 1955]

Blackley, Lachlan, *Wallpaper*, London: Laurence King, 2006

Bordo, Susan, 'Never Just Pictures' in *The Feminism and Visual Culture Reader*, edited by Amelia Jones, London and New York: Routledge, 2003, pp.454–66

Busch, Akiko, *Geography of Home: Writings about Where We Live*, New York: Princeton Architectural Press, 1999

Butler, Judith, 'Performative Acts and Gender Constitution: An Essay in Phenomenology and Feminist Theory', *Theatre Journal*, vol.40, no.4, December 1988

Butler, Judith, *Gender Trouble: Feminism and the Subversion of Identity*, New York and London: Routledge, 1990; 2nd edition, 1999

Calloway, Stephen, *Twentieth-century Decoration: The Domestic Interior from 1900 to the Present Day*, London: Weidenfeld and Nicolson, and New York: Rizzoli, 1988

Collings, Matthew, *Sarah Lucas*, London: Tate Publishing, 2002

Cooper, Nicholas, *The Opulent Eye: Late Victorian and Edwardian Taste in Interior Design*, photographic plates by H. Bedford Lemere, London: Architectural Press, 1976; New York: Watson Guptill, 1977

Crick, Clare, *Historic Wallpapers in the Whitworth Art Gallery*, Manchester: Whitworth Art Gallery, 1972

De Salvo, Donna M. (editor), *Apocalyptic Wallpaper: Robert Gober, Abigail Lane, Virgil Marti, and Andy Warhol* (exhibition catalogue), Columbus, Ohio: Wexner Center for the Arts, Ohio State University, 1997

Dewling, David (editor), *Home and Garden: Paintings and Drawings of English, Middle-class, Urban Domestic Spaces 1675–1914* (exhibition catalogue), London: Geffrye Museum, 2003

Entwisle, E. A., *A Literary History of Wallpaper*, London: Batsford, 1960

Entwisle, E. A., *Wallpapers of the Victorian Era*, Leigh-on-Sea, Essex: F. Lewis, 1964

Entwisle, E. A., *The Book of Wallpaper: A History and an Appreciation*, revised edition, Bath: Kingsmead, 1970

Entwisle, E. A., *French Scenic Wallpapers 1800–1860*, Leigh-on-Sea, Essex: F. Lewis, 1972

Felski, Rita, *The Gender of Modernity*, Cambridge, MA: Harvard University Press, 1995

Flood, Richard, Gary Garrels and Ann Temkin, *Robert Gober: Sculpture + Drawing*, Minneapolis: Walker Art Center, 1999

Foster, Susan Leigh, 'The Ballerina's Phallic Pointe' in *The Feminism and Visual Culture Reader*, edited by Amelia Jones, London and New York: Routledge, 2003, pp.434–54

Fowler, John and John Cornforth, *English Decoration in the 18th Century*, London, Barrie and Jenkins, and Princeton, NJ: Pyne Press, 1974; 2nd edition, Barrie and Jenkins, 1978

Garrett, Elisabeth Donaghy, *At Home: The American Family 1750–1870*, New York: Abrams, 1990

Gere, Charlotte, *Nineteenth-Century Decoration: The Art of the Interior*, London: Weidenfeld and Nicolson, and New York: Abrams, 1989

Gere, Charlotte and Lesley Hoskins, *The House Beautiful: Oscar Wilde and the Aesthetic Interior*, London: Lund Humphries in association with the Geffrye Museum, 2000

Gilman, Charlotte Perkins, *The Yellow Wallpaper and Selected Writings*, London: Virago, 2009

Groom, Simon (editor), *Niki de Sainte Phalle*, London: Tate Publishing, 2008

Hapgood, Marilyn Oliver, *Wallpaper and the Artist: From Dürer to Warhol*, New York: Abbeville Press, 1992

Hoskins, Lesley (editor), *The Papered Wall: The History, Patterns and Techniques of Wallpaper*, London: Thames and Hudson, and New York: Abrams, 1994; revised edition, Thames and Hudson, 2005

Huyssen, Andreas, *After the Great Divide: Modernism, Mass Culture, Postmodernism*, Bloomington: Indiana University Press, 1986; London: Macmillan, 1988

Hyde, Sarah, *Exhibiting Gender*, Manchester: Manchester University Press, 1997

Jacqué, Bernard, *Papier peint & revolution*, Rixheim: Musée du Papier Peint, 1989

Jacqué, Bernard (editor), *Les Papiers peints en arabesques de la fin du XVIII siècle*, Paris: Martinière/Rixheim: Musée du Papier Peint, 1995

Jones, Amelia (editor), *The Feminism and Visual Culture Reader*, London and New York: Routledge, 2003

Keeble, Trevor, 'Fabricating the Domestic Surface: A Very Brief History of an Old Problem' in *Lost Narratives: The Work of Catherine Bertola*, edited by Jon Bewley, Sunderland: Art Editions North, 2005

Kirkham, Pat (editor), *The Gendered Object*, Manchester: Manchester University Press, 1996

Kosuda-Warner, Joanne, *Kitsch to Corbusier: Wallpapers from the 1950s* (exhibition catalogue), New York: Cooper-Hewitt National Design Museum, 1995

Kosuda-Warner, Joanne, *Landscape Wallcoverings*, London: Scala/New York: Cooper-Hewitt National Design Museum, 2001

Kracauer, Siegfried, *The Mass Ornament: Weimar Essays*, edited by Thomas Y. Levin, Cambridge, MA: Harvard University Press, 1995

Lynn, Catherine, *Wallpaper in America: From the Seventeenth Century to World War I*, New York: Norton, 1980

Möller, Werner, '"No Risk, No Gain": Strategies for the Bauhaus Wallpaper' in *Rasch Buch/book 1897–1997*, Bramsche: Rasch, 1998, pp.110–27

Mulvey, Laura, 'You Don't Know What is Happening, Do You, Mr Jones?', *Spare Rib*, no.8, 1973, pp.127–31

Nesbitt, Judith (editor), *Robert Gober* (exhibition catalogue), London: Serpentine Gallery, and Liverpool: Tate Gallery, 1993

Nouvel, Odile, *Wall-papers of France 1800–1850*, translated by Margaret Timmers, London: Zwemmer, and New York: Rizzoli, 1981

Nouvel-Kammerer, Odile (editor), *French Scenic Wallpaper 1790–1865*, revised edition, Paris: Flammarion, 2000 [originally published as *Papiers peints panoramiques*, 1990]

Nylander, Richard C., Elizabeth Redmond and Penny J. Sander (editors), *Wallpaper in New England*, Boston: Society for the Preservation of New England Antiquities, 1986

Oman, Charles C. and Jean Hamilton, *Wallpapers: A History and Illustrated Catalogue of the Collection of the Victoria and Albert Museum*, London: Sotheby Publications in association with the Victoria and Albert Museum, 1982

Painter, Colin (editor), *Contemporary Art and the Home*, Oxford and New York: Berg, 2002

Parry, Linda (editor), *William Morris*, London: Philip Wilson in association with the Victoria and Albert Museum, and New York: Abrams, 1996

A Popular Art: British Wallpapers 1930–1960 (exhibition catalogue, Silver Studio Collection), London: Middlesex Polytechnic, 1989

Reed, Christopher (editor), *Not at Home: The Suppression of Domesticity in Modern Art and Architecture*, London: Thames and Hudson, 1996

Rogers, Mary F., *Barbie Culture*, London: Sage, 1999

Rosoman, Treve, *London Wallpapers: Their Manufacture and Use 1690–1840*, London: English Heritage, 1992

Saumarez Smith, Charles, *Eighteenth-Century Decoration: Design and the Domestic Interior in England*, London: Weidenfeld and Nicolson, and New York: Abrams, 1993

Saunders, Gill, *Wallpaper in Interior Decoration*, London: V&A Publications, 2002

Sparke, Penny, *As Long as It's Pink: The Sexual Politics of Taste*, London: Pandora, 1995

Sugden, A.V. and J.L. Edmondson, *A History of English Wallpaper 1509–1914*, London: Batsford, and New York: Scribner, 1926

Tannenbaum, Judith and Marion Boulton Stroud, *On the Wall: Contemporary Wallpaper* (exhibition catalogue), Providence: Rhode Island School of Design Museum of Art, and Philadelphia: Fabric Workshop and Museum, 2003

Teynac, Françoise, Pierre Nolot and Jean-Denis Vivien, *Wallpaper: A History*, London: Thames and Hudson, and New York: Rizzoli, 1982

Thomas Demand (includes essay by Beatriz Colomina and a conversation between Alexander Kluge and Thomas Demand), London: Serpentine Gallery/Munich: Schirmer Mosel, 2006

Thornton, Peter, *Seventeenth-century Interior Decoration in England, France and Holland*, New Haven and London: Yale University Press, 1978

Thornton, Peter, *Authentic Décor: The Domestic Interior 1620–1920*, London: Weidenfeld and Nicolson, and New York: Viking, 1984

Turner, Mark and Lesley Hoskins, *Silver Studio of Design: A Design and Source Book for Home Decoration*, Exeter: Webb and Bower, 1988; revised edition, Leicester: Magna, 1995

Wells-Cole, Anthony, *Historic Paper Hangings from Temple Newsam and Other English Houses* (Temple Newsam Country House Studies 1), Leeds: Leeds City Art Galleries, 1983

Wolff, Janet, 'The Feminine in Modern Art: Benjamin, Simmel and the Gender of Modernity' in *Theory, Culture and Society*, vol.17, no.6, 2000, pp.33–53

Woods, Christine (editor), *Sanderson 1860–1985* (exhibition catalogue), London: Arthur Sanderson and Sons, 1985

Index

Author Biographies

Gill Saunders, Senior Curator of Prints at the Victoria and Albert Museum, is internationally renowned for her expertise on wallpaper, contemporary art, particularly printmaking, and installation. Her publications include *Apocalyptic Wallpaper* (1997), *Wallpaper in Interior Decoration* (2002) and *Prints Now: Directions and Definitions* (with Rosie Miles; 2006). She has organized many exhibitions and displays at the V&A, most recently *Mapping the Imagination* (2008). In 2009 she was one of the selectors for the inaugural Northern Print Biennale. She continues to publish, lecture and broadcast on a wide range of print-related topics.

Christine Woods, Curator (Wallpapers) at the Whitworth Art Gallery, The University of Manchester, has an international reputation in the field of 19th- and 20th-century wallpaper history. She has lectured and published widely on the subject and, drawing on the Whitworth's extensive collection, has organized numerous exhibitions of historic and modern wallpapers and other wallcoverings. She is a founder member of the Wallpaper History Society and Editor of its triennial journal, *The Wallpaper History Review.*

Dominique Heyse-Moore, Assistant Curator (Textiles & Wallpapers) at the Whitworth Art Gallery, has a background in design history. Her research focuses on the ways in which design relates to the construction of identities. She has worked in museums and galleries in Manchester for the past three years on several projects, including *Revealing Histories: Remembering Slavery.*

Trevor Keeble teaches Design History in the Faculty of Art, Design & Architecture at Kingston University, London. He is an Associate Director of the Modern Interiors Research Centre (MIRC) and his work focuses upon design, domesticity and homemaking. He is currently co-writing *Design: An Interdisciplinary Introduction. Designing the Modern Interior,* a collection of essays co-edited with colleagues from MIRC, was published in 2009.